Spiritual Chemistry

The Interaction of Spiritual Energy
with the Physical World

Malcolm K. Smith, Ph.D.

Malcolm K. Smith

SEPTEMBER, 2010

Spiritual Chemistry:
The Interaction of Spiritual Energy with the Physical World

ISBN 10: 1-933817-58-5
ISBN 13: 978-1-933817-58-3

Cover design provided by Susan Reed.
Editing assistance provided by Rebecca Hanna.

Published by: Profits Publishing
http://profitspublishing.com

Canadian Address
1265 Charter Hill Drive
Coquitlam, BC, V3E 1P1
Phone: (604) 941-3041
Fax: (604) 944-7993

US Address
1300 Boblett Street
Unit A-218
Blaine, WA 98230
Phone: (866) 492-6623
Fax: (250) 493-6603

Book Dedication

For Beth who created a five-dimensional space in which I could write this book.

Acknowledgments

I must acknowledge the contributions of my human guides to the spiritual realms. Alannah Jantzen and Susan Harris showed me pathways I never knew existed and explained what we had seen on our adventures. My artist friend and co-researcher Michelle DeMello showed me how the spiritual world of artistic inspiration becomes reality. When the time came to put it all down on paper Ann Perrick joined them as they helped me make my first few faltering steps. Throughout all the writing Dawn Stewart has been a tireless editor helping me say what it is I really mean.

Klaus Monies has been an invaluable source for illustration suggestions throughout the whole project. I am glad that we were able to include seven of his diagrams in the final book.

Thank you my dear human friends.

Contents

Introduction

When I first started writing this book I intended it to be about my psychic experiences. But soon it became apparent that beings in other dimensions – Angels and spirit guides – had other plans for it. After reviewing information I received by channeling, I realized that I was writing about spiritual energy and its interaction with the physical world. The information I was given seemed very relevant to this particular time on planet Earth with its mysteries such as crop formations, light orbs in digital photos and images miraculously appearing on a variety of surfaces. If you find these mysteries interesting then I think you will find this book interesting. It offers explanations, not only of the above phenomena, but of miracles that occur in our human bodies and in the natural world of which most of us are not even aware.

This is not one of those books that suggest spiritual rules to live by. Other people – like Wayne Dyer – do a great job in that direction. Rather this is a 'The Way Things Work' type of book, but it's different in that it describes the way <u>spiritual</u> things work. Being trained as a chemist, I have been called upon by Angels and my Guides to meld my physical science with their spiritual science. I am asked to explain – as simply as possible – a number of things that have been puzzling humans for some time. For example, how does the spirit of a new born child enter its body and guide it to grow into an adult human? Or where in the human body does the spirit reside and how does it operate that fantastic computer we call a brain? Or how do the molecules we eat in our food get converted into living tissue?

So far I have been talking to spiritual people or workers for the light – they know who they are. But now, fellow scientists, I've got a special message for you! Science doesn't make sense without God – which in my book equals Spirit with a capital S. I know you like definitions, here's one from the Angels: "Spirit is energy aware of itself." In all our bodies we humans have some of that self-aware energy. We refer to it as our spirit that is a little part of Spirit. It returns to other dimensions when the body dies.

Do you realize, scientists – yes I'm still talking to you – that in this universe, in which we find ourselves, there's a whole culture of spiritual energy science? Beings in hyper-dimensions – dimensions 5 through 12 which include most extra-terrestrials – know how to manipulate spiritual energy. Our physics is lagging behind what is generally known in the universe because of the research methods we use. Our statements of physics and chemistry concepts in mathematics have worked well for us. But this technique is running into roadblocks. It's becoming increasingly difficult to interpret the mathematical results as physical mechanisms – think of Schrodinger's cat! Furthermore, we do not know how to put spiritual energy concepts into mathematics. This reminds us of the divide between what we do in our work and what we hear in church. It's time for help from our siblings in other dimensions.

A few authors have asked for help from our hyper-dimensional siblings. Most of us are familiar with channeled fiction books like *Jonathan Livingston Seagull*. In the area of non-fiction, one author* asked for help from them in finding information about twelfth-century ideas and concepts that explained puzzling events in the history of the Knights Templar. Unwittingly I have stumbled into the same mode of research. I see in this approach that I have been given by the Angels a new research tool and a whole new way to view our human existence on the surface of planet Earth.

I invite you to join me in talking to the Angels. Maybe we will find answers to the really big questions – such as "Why are we here?"

Malcolm K. Smith / October 18, 2009

---

*   Juan Garcia Atienza, *The Knights Templar in the Golden Age of Spain*

CHAPTER 1: I'm Reality Challenged Too, How About You?

In This Chapter:

- *How I Met My Guides – Childhood Years*
- *Farnborough – I Hear Them*
- *Manchester-University and the Guardian of the Threshold*
- *Working With My Guides*
- *Guide Changes*
- *How I Get My Information*
- *Automatic Writing*
- *Pendulum*
- *Channeling*
- *Other Methods*
- *Books*

How I Met My Guides – Childhood Years

I was born November, 1936, in Portsmouth, England, so I was almost three years old when the war started. Living in Portsmouth at that time was dangerous because the navy dockyard there was a prime bombing target. Like many kids of my age, I was evacuated. My mother and I were billeted on a small farm run by Mr. and Mrs. Glasspool in the Meon Valley about thirty miles outside Portsmouth.

I was an only child and, since there were no other kids in the immediate neighborhood, I had nobody to play with. Instead, I had two imaginary playmates that I called Joe and Bob. The three of us used to turn Mr. Glasspool's old armchair into a steam locomotive and hurtle it down the track at breakneck speed. My mother used to smile benignly at these antics. I think she knew then what I have come to realize: that these playmates were my Spirit Guides. (It wasn't until 1980 that I found their real names were Ulrigh and Lester, friends from previous lifetimes.) My mother was very wise in the ways of Spirit and she told me that I had the same gift. From the

1

age of three I knew things by extrasensory means and my mother encouraged me to talk about such things.

As the war finished we moved back into Portsmouth and I transferred from the little village school, where I had been since 1941, to a big state elementary school in the city. From there I passed the '11 plus' examination, with the help of my father's coaching, so that in 1948 I started attending one of the three 'grammar' (secondary) schools in Portsmouth. The grammar schools were intended to prepare some percentage of the students, about 25 percent in my school's case, for university. The process of picking out likely university students, called 'streaming' into A, B, C and D categories, started in the first few days at the school. After about a week to get organized, we were given examinations in English, Arithmetic and Puzzles – the latter was an intelligence test in disguise.

The occasion of these streaming examinations was the first time my Guides gave me assistance that was obvious, even to an eleven-year-old boy. In the arithmetic test I was shown diagrams in my head which made it clear how to calculate the answers. The puzzles were all just like the ones my Dad had me practice for the '11 plus' exam. And the English was a breeze: write an essay and two verses of a poem – things that I had been doing for years at the elementary school. (In 1980 I found out that my Guide Lester had been my English teacher in a previous lifetime!) I was not surprised to find that I had 'aced' the exams and I was put into the 'A' stream, heading for university.

After that experience I began to realize I had powerful help nearby and I paid attention to what that help told me. Things like, "Never smoke cigarettes" and "Start long distance running," plus "You are going to need this body for a long time – make it strong." I did all the things that were suggested. But none of these things came to me consciously; it was as if they were just thoughts that came to me in a sort of dream.

At grammar school, another gift came to me – science. One of my elementary school teachers, Mr. Knight, had demonstrated an

2

experiment he found in a book. We turned lime water milky by blowing our breath through a straw into it. I was the only kid in the class that wanted to know why the lime water turned milky and I pestered poor Mr. Knight with my questions, "Why, why, why?" Unfortunately he never studied science and couldn't explain the reaction. Now here I was at the grammar school actually having science lessons from teachers who all knew why lime water turns milky when it is mixed with carbon dioxide from our breath. (A precipitate of calcium carbonate is formed -MKS.)

Later I realized this experience had been planted by my Guides in their subtle way to ensure I followed my planned life path, which led to my becoming a scientist.

As I progressed through the grammar school I was aware of the help that was available to me from some source that I never personified. I came to know that if I had a problem, all I had to do was sit quietly and I would be shown how to go about getting the answer. I was never given the answer itself, only suggestions for the route to it. And all this help seemed to come as thoughts in a dreamy disconnected way.

Farnborough – I Hear Them

The first time I actually heard a voice from my Guides, it saved my life. I was at the 1952 Farnborough Air Show with my school friend Brian. We were standing on the lower slope of a little hill which was crowded with people trying to get a better view of the runways. Overhead the new de Havilland 110 fighter aircraft had just gone through the sound barrier and the air show commentator had remarked on the unusual puffs of smoke that came from the plane with the shock wave as the speed of sound was exceeded. A few minutes later the DH110 was back making a fast, low-level run across the airfield toward the crowd. Suddenly the plane reared up on its tail and the fuselage seemed to be punched out of the wings; we saw the parts of the plane spiraling down onto the runway like sycamore seeds. Then in front and above us we became aware of the plane's two engines, which had burst through the wreckage and were now lazily spinning toward us with pieces of pipe flying off in all directions. One engine was higher and seemed to be passing over us, but the other was coming straight for us.

That was the first time I heard a loud voice in my head. It said, "Run that way." Shouting, "This way" to Brian, I ran as fast as my legs would carry me to the side – the direction I 'knew' was intended by the owner of the voice. As I ran, I planned to dive to the ground before the engine hit because I thought it was going to explode. But after a few seconds I felt a shock and knew it had already impacted the hill. I turned and saw the hill covered in smashed bodies and blood. Out of the crowd of survivors came Brian. He was safe! He had been knocked over by people who fell on him. Shaking like leaves, we went to the car park and sat on the bus until it left for home. Later that day I realized I had Guides who spoke to me. They had saved me from sharing death with the thirty-eight people who perished on that little hill where we had been standing.

Manchester-University and the Guardian of the Threshold

In 1955 I graduated from the grammar school with sufficiently high marks to be able to go to university. Because I wanted to study polymers, which was a developing field of chemistry at that time, I selected a degree course in Textile Chemistry at the University of Manchester Institute of Science and Technology (UMIST). I graduated with honors in 1958 and was accepted to do research in physical organic chemistry with Dr. G. Egerton at UMIST. That research resulted in a Ph.D. in 1961.

All through my university days, my Guides helped in my studies. They helped me find library references quickly. They helped me predict four out of the five final degree exam questions. They saved me from losing my eyesight in a laboratory explosion and they helped me invent pieces of equipment I needed for my research.
Here's an example of the latter guidance. I needed to collect – for chemical analysis – crystals so small that they could only be seen

4

under a microscope. One evening, with that problem in mind, I settled into a comfortable seat on a train for the twenty-five-minute ride to Marple Bridge, Cheshire, where I lived at that time. I dozed in the warmth of the train into a kind of trance, a trance in which I was shown a tiny vacuum cleaner powered with water pump suction. By the time I got off the train in Marple I had the apparatus design clear in my mind. The next day, I made the vacuum cleaner out of glass tubing with a suction orifice less than half a millimeter in diameter. Working under a low-power microscope, I could put the orifice over each crystal, break it away from the surface with a small movement and it was sucked through alcohol where it dissolved to make the solution I needed for analysis. Thank you Guides!

During my days in Manchester I was introduced to a supernatural being other than my Guides. In my undergraduate days I shared an apartment with Rick, an engineering student. One foggy Friday night, I was alone because Rick had left earlier to stay with his girlfriend. I sat in one of the two single beds in the room reading an article in *Reader's Digest* about a ship that had nearly capsized during a night of a terrible storm. In the morning, the crew came on deck and saw that the ship's mast had been bent at a crazy angle. They thought that the hand of God had reached down and saved the ship from turning over by holding the mast.

I switched off the light and sat there in the dim light of a street lamp filtering through the fog. I looked over to Rick's bed where, five hours earlier, he had stood his big, square briefcase, heavy with textbooks. I must have been feeling very materialistic at that time, because I thought about the *Reader's Digest* article, "What a load of rubbish! Why, it's like expecting Rick's briefcase to move." Instantly, the briefcase fell over onto its side. I was terrified! But what impressed me more than the bag's movement was the wonderful feeling of calm that descended over me like a reassuring blanket of love. I then became aware of a great black rectangular figure standing in one corner of the room. The figure was as dark as a black hole, the weak light from the street lamp seemed to be absorbed by it. As I watched, the figure grew in height until it towered about twenty feet through the roof out into the night. It never spoke, but telepathically it told me of great love that was available to us all and work I should do in this life. I was completely reassured and calm. I laid down in bed and fell asleep immediately.

Thirty years later I read *Spiritwalker* by Hank Wesselman (Ref. 1-1). In this spiritual anthropology book were ancient pictographs painted on canyon walls in the American Southwest, Figure 1-1. I recognized in the pictographs the tall black figure that had appeared to me that foggy night in Manchester. It was, I read, what many native people call the Guardian of the Threshold, the threshold into other dimensions of existence.

Working With My Guides

Most of my working time has been spent in industrial research centres doing applied research. It was applied in different kinds of production plants, especially paper mills. An important part of that kind of work is solving problems quickly. ("We don't want it ASAP, Malcolm; we want it yesterday!")

I found I could walk into a production plant and my Guides would tell me what the problem was and the best approach to solving it. For example, when I was consulting in more recent times, I was called to a paper coating mill that had just started production. As the production manager walked me to the coating machine he told me the coating would not stick to the paper. As we reached the machine, I was shown in my head the cause of the problem. Within three hours I had the coating reformulated and the process running smoothly. Thank you Guides!

I have read in *Notes from the Cosmos* by electronics engineer Gordon Michael Scallion (Ref. 1-2) that he had a similar gift. He could look at a complex group of circuits and tell which would work and, if not, where the problem components were.

Guide Changes

During the 1980s and 90s I became aware my Guides were changing. While Ulrigh stayed with me, Lester left and was replaced by

6

Andrea. Early in the 1990s in England, my cousin Irene died and a dear friend and ex-colleague, Vaughan, died suddenly. In Hawaii another friend, Helen, died. Within about three years all had joined my Guides; their arrival was announced in dreams. It seemed my Guides were increasing in number in preparation for some future event.

In early 1997 I was reading alone late one night; all the rest of my family were asleep. Suddenly I heard quite clearly in my left ear, "Malcolm, we want you to retire and come and work with us." After some wrangling with family and my employer, I did as my Guides had asked me. I set up a consulting firm to continue my technical work – and it was just as well I did, because the research centre where I had been working was suddenly closed down seven months later. While I continued my chemistry consulting I also prepared to give metaphysical talks. My new career had begun.

Since the time I made that decision my Guides have steadily increased in number until now; I currently have seventeen working with me. They consist of school friends, work acquaintances, and people I don't remember meeting, at least not in this lifetime. They all specialize in some aspect of my life and the work we do together. I will explain their functions in Chapter 3. Meanwhile, I want to let them have the last word in this section:

In distant days we were informed of Malcolm's life plan.
We all volunteered to come and help his worthy cause.
So we joined his existing guides in the 90s.
Now we all work as special topic advisors to our dear Malcolm.

How I Get My Information

As you will have seen from the last section, I have been in touch with my Spirit Guides for many years. Once I realized they were with me and ready to talk to me – in the late 1970s – I started to connect with them at least once a month. Since about 2004 I have also been given information by a group of Angels. I will tell you about their contacts shortly.

Automatic Writing

At first I was shown that I could do automatic writing. At that time I was working as a research chemist in a forest products firm in Canada. One day at work I was writing a report (longhand in those days!). Suddenly I realized that I had written a couple of pages that had no connection with the report. Instead, it seemed to be about spiritual matters. Reading over it I realized that I had fallen into an altered mental state and had written the pages without remembering. I wrote at the top of the first page, "Automatic writing!" and put it in a new file that was to grow steadily over the next few years.

About this time I started to go to meetings with people who were more psychic than I was. The psychics, nearly all women, usually used a Ouija board to channel information from the 'other side' as they called it. From them I learned a lot about the other side, or the 5th dimension as I now prefer to call it. Part of the information was about my Guides, who they were and the previous lifetimes we had together.

My automatic writing continued and I realized it came from my Guides. The information became more focused and I started getting material that I could present at the meetings. Some of this material was in the form of poems, like the one in the box on this page. (Lester was one of my Guides at that time.) During one of the meetings I was told by the psychics that one day I would be teaching people about this 'weird stuff' as I referred to it then.

> **Who would have thought a little while ago**
> **Of the many things you would come to know.**
> **Who would have dreamed of hearts filled with love**
> **When as a small boy you opened your glove**
> **And found your heart hiding there.**
>
> **LESTER; 1 March, 1983**

8

About this time, early 1980s, the weird stuff seemed to get weirder. That hint about teaching it one day made me start to question what I was receiving through the automatic writing and the psychics. I felt I just couldn't believe what I was being told about teaching and even writing books on spiritual matters. I guessed that my subconscious was doing a little wishful thinking and leading me to these incredible news items. So I announced, out loud, to my Guides that I was beginning to doubt the truth of what I was receiving. The next batch of automatic writing told me to get a pendulum and some sort of letter chart that they could use to spell out words. The Guides announced that I would regard this as a tool that was not connected to my mind and so should find it easier to believe.

Pendulum

I got a pendulum (in an odd way that I will tell you about in Chapter 3). I made a circular chart with thirty-six pie slice segments (twenty-six letters and ten numbers) and I was ready to roll. At first it was tough to get any sense out of this tool – I think I was trying too hard. After experimenting with different approaches, I found one that worked was to imagine the colours of the rainbow (ROYGBIV) as I swung the pendulum over the chart. That seemed to occupy my conscious mind and, eventually, we laboriously spelled out words via the pendulum.

With constant practice, which for the last ten years has been every day, the process has become quite fast. For example, on the next page, the poem "Forty Four" took about one and a half hours to transmit. "Crystal Light" was the name I was given at the end of the poem and I thought it was a name my group of Guides had chosen. However, as I have written this book I have discovered that it is the name of a group of Angels who have been helping me since about 2003 when we wrote the poem "Forty Four." I asked my Guides about this and they told me:

The Angels were speaking on our behalf in the poem.
We cooperate with the Angels in helping humans.
We are one big team.
Teamwork is essential in bringing the word to humans.

Forty Four

Slipping, sliding, scurrying they come,
Running, rushing, rumbling they go,
Pushing, probing, propelling their wants,
Taking, baking, making their plans.

All men are anxious to wear the crown of power.
Under a mask of baleful smiles
Lives of anger are put into valueless gear.
Many come to Earth with plans of gold,
Valued highly as they leave the fold.
Soon the plan of life is lost,
Soon the physical world removes intent.

There is no question that cannot be answered.
Remove the fear and call your guides.
We are waiting for that voice that wonders:
"Anybody out there?"
"Anyone without a body?"
"Show us the path we planned to walk."
"Think I could do something with this life?"
"Remember me? We played together when I was a child."
"Thought you might like to come out and play again,
Even though I'm forty four!"

We are here, waiting for your call.
We can help you find your lost path,
Recover those lost golden plans,
Survive the cancer, turn it into understanding,
Recover your joy at the thrill of life.
Who but your guides know
Your secret answers to these questions?

Soon you will see a coincidence.
That is our sign, it means we are here.
We love you and want to hear from you.
Please go inside your head and call.
We will answer to any name you choose,
An answer will be yours.
The voice you hear will be ours.
Then we can all go out to play again,
Even though you're forty four.

CRYSTAL LIGHT; 7 July, 2003

10

Channeling

I have friends that can channel in beautiful clear words that inspire. I never thought I would be able to do that. But one day I was running the pendulum and, instead of remembering the words to write down later, I was dictating them to a friend. I noticed that with my memory inactive I was free to explore other sensations around this experience. I noticed that I 'knew' the words that were coming next. In the messages I received that day was one saying that I didn't really need the pendulum, at least not all the time.

A couple of days later, as I started to run the pendulum, I was told to put it away and just talk into a recorder. I did some deep breathing, meditated on colours of the rainbow, until I went into a light trance and then I just talked into the recorder. About half an hour later when I listened to the tape I realized that although I was aware of the general topic I had described I did not remember a lot of the details. So that is my mode of channeling now. Of course I have to transcribe the tapes, and I find it best to do that right away or I lose some of the feeling of the transmission.

My channeling is reserved for when the Angels or my Guides want to transmit big blocks of descriptive information, for example, the communications in Appendices 2 through 10. We still use the pendulum in the following situations:

- When available time is short, which is usually the case for the daily chat.
- When specific information is being transmitted, e.g., the information on zero point energy in Appendix 1.
- When we are discussing something and I have a lot of questions, e.g., on specific past life relationships.
- When I want to check some outrageous things that I have been told in the channeling. Often in the form, "Are you seriously suggesting that I should ... etc."
- When my Guides want to make jokes and puns in the messages or give me unexpected word combinations. They

often do this to emphasize that the material is not coming from my subconscious.

In connection with the last two points above, my Guides want me to tell you that this conveying of information between dimensions is not a serious process. Just because they are dead, from our point of view, they are not solemn. They regard humour as a great gift from God. They say, *It lubricates the interactions between beings in different dimensions.* For example, once I had just understood some obscure science connection and they said, *Eggsactly – you catch on quite fast for a human!*

Other Methods

In this section I want to mention two other methods of connecting with other dimensions.

The first I call computer meditation. When my Guides had convinced me that I could channel by speaking into a recorder, it became obvious that transcribing was the time consuming step. To help me through this, they suggested that I sit at my computer keyboard and type the words straight into memory. But it didn't work because my keyboarding was too slow; I couldn't keep up with the flow of words coming into my head. I had to go back to the voice recorder. But I want to stress that for people with fast keyboarding skills, this is probably the best way to channel into print.

The second is running meditation. I have been running since I was twelve years old. Currently, I run five kilometers two or three times per week. I found some time ago that I often received information during the second half of my run. It seemed that when my conscious mind was occupied with the physiological changes in my body, especially deep breathing, my spiritual receivers opened to the universe. In her book *The Psychic Power of Running* (Ref. 1-3), Valerie Andrews gives accounts of how some primitive cultures raise this form of meditation to a powerful healing process.

Books

For as long as I have been aware of beings in other dimensions, I have read books that I thought might help me to understand their intermittent influence in my life. This need was particularly strong when I had strange experiences – like the visit from the Guardian of the Threshold described previously in this chapter. I really looked for help and understanding and I believe that, as I did, it came to me in unexpected ways. But I never feared that I was crazy; it just didn't occur to me that some people would think I was. I guess I am too confident in my beliefs and powers of observation – some might say obstinate – to think that these strange experiences were signs of impending mental illness.

In the 1950s in England, books on psychic matters were not common. At least where I lived there were no bookshops specializing in metaphysical books as there are now in North America. I found some reports sponsored by the British Society for Psychical Research but to my young taste their concentration on physical proof seemed rather boring. Two books I remember helping significantly were *The Haunting of Borely Rectory* (Ref. 1-4) and *Gildas Communicates* (Ref. 1-5). I think at that time Edgar Cayce and J.B. Rhine were well-known authors, particularly in North America, but my inefficient search did not find their works.

About 1970 I returned to England after a few years working in Australia and Canada. By that time books on metaphysical topics were starting to become more popular and I found one that really set me on my present course. It was *The Infinite Hive* written by Rosalind Heywood in 1964 (Ref. 1-6). I rushed through this book saying many times, "Yes, yes, I know that feeling." At last, it seemed I had found someone who had experienced strange events and influences like mine. At the same time my confidence in the existence of unseen intelligent influences in our lives was boosted by discussions with some of my colleagues at the research centre where I worked near London.

13

In early 1974 I returned to Canada to work as a research chemist in a forest products company in Vancouver, BC. Almost as soon as I arrived I found a book published just over a year earlier. This was *Seth Speaks* channeled by Jane Roberts during the 1960s (Ref. 1-7). Here at last was a systematic explanation by a discarnate entity of life in different dimensions and their relationship to ours. In my opinion, Jane Roberts's books launched the New Age as we know it today. I read all the Seth books and others Jane Roberts had written without Seth's help such as the *Oversoul Seven* series (Ref. 1-8).

Some other significant books came out in the early 1970s, for example the *Don Juan* series by Carlos Casteneda (Ref. 1-9). Richard Bach wrote *Jonathan Livingston Seagull* (Ref. 1-10) through a process similar to channeling. Ruth Montgomery wrote several books, such as *Strangers Among Us* (Ref. 1-11) by dictation from her group of Guides. I feel very close to Ruth Montgomery since her method of writing parallels my own. As we moved into the 1980s, the number of channeled books increased. Ramtha was channeled by J.Z. Knight (Ref. 1-12) and Lazaris by Jach Pursel (Ref. 1-13). I found all these books full of practical spiritual wisdom. They made the spiritual life seem reasonable, attainable by ordinary people and not just by holy people living in remote places. For me this was the dawning of the Age of Aquarius.

In spite of the joyful feelings this knowledge gave me, I still felt this world view was incomplete; the new spiritual world did not relate to science. Yet I knew from my experiences in science and invention that unseen Guides had a hand in bringing new technical things to the Earth. (I will talk about this in greater detail in the chapter on creativity.) Then one day after one of my 'Edge of Reality' talks in the 1990s, a lady came to me at the end of the class and handed me a book saying, "You are meant to read this." I opened the book randomly and there on the open page was an answer to a question that had been bothering me for some time. I was hooked! That book was *Alchemy of the Human Spirit* (a chemist couldn't have a better keyword than *alchemy*) by Kryon, who referred to himself as a magnetic master, channeled through Lee Carroll (Ref. 1-14), an audio engineer. I was hooked to the nth degree!

The Kryon books consist mainly of a clear explanation of the way the universe works and how humans relate to it and the beings that inhabit it. Kryon explains these things and the power of love in simple terms, often in the form of analogies and parables. These books were what I had been looking for over the years. There are currently (early 2009) eleven books in the series. I have read, and reread, every one and I attend every Kryon seminar that is presented in the Vancouver area. You will find that I have been greatly influenced by Kryon because I resonate with his explanations, parables and love.

You may be wondering, if Kryon is so great, why I find it necessary to write another spiritual science book. I wondered the same thing myself. But as I understand it from my Guides, there is a need for a book about chemistry and spiritual energy. I asked my Guides about this and here's what they said:

We appreciate your concerns but your book is necessary because others do not have chemistry.
Chemistry is where Spirit interacts with the physical.

Now as I write this, you can go into any one of many metaphysical bookstores and feel overwhelmed by the vast amount of material available. There's even more on the Internet! In selecting books, I advise you to trust your own discernment. Listen to your inner voice and read what draws you and feels right for you.

In writing this book I recognize that many ideas and explanations which were in my head probably came from all the books that I have talked about above, and more. I have also dipped into other specialized books. Wherever I know that I am using an idea from another author I give that person credit by name. But I am aware that many of these ideas may become modified by input from other dimensions until the source is untraceable. I ask for forgiveness if I have unknowingly offended any authors in this way.

When I was working for various technical organizations I always had to give answers in quantified form. ("We need numbers,

Malcolm, not vague hand waving!") So it is my habit to guesstimate the contributions to my finished talks from various sources. So here goes for this book:

- Automatic writing – 10%
- Pendulum – 25%
- Channeling – 25%
- Other people's books – 35%

I know that doesn't add to 100 percent; there's an outstanding 5 percent. That is the material that I have learned from people I have met or who have come to my classes bringing their wonderful stories of events that they and their families have experienced. I thank them all and send them any blessings that are mine to give.

References for Chapter 1

Ref. 1-1   *Spiritwalker – Messages from the Future* by Hank Wesselman

Ref. 1-2   *Notes from the Cosmos* by Gordon-Michael Scallion

Ref. 1-3   *The Psychic Power of Running* by Valerie Andrews

Ref. 1-4   *The Haunting of Borely Rectory* by Eric J. Dingwall, Kathleen M. Goldney and Trevor H. Hall

Ref. 1-5   *Gildas Communicates* by Ruth White and Mary Swainson

Ref. 1-6   *The Infinite Hive* by Rosalind Heywood

Ref. 1-7   *Seth Speaks* by Jane Roberts

Ref. 1-8   *The Education of Oversoul 7* by Jane Roberts

Ref. 1-9   *A Separate Reality* by Carlos Casteneda

Ref. 1-10   *Jonathan Livingston Seagull* by Richard Bach

Ref. 1-11   *Strangers Among Us* by Ruth Montgomery

Ref. 1-12   *Ramtha – Voyage to the New World* by J.Z. Knight and D.J. Mahr

Ref. 1-13   *Lazaris – The Sacred Journey* by Jach Pursel

Ref. 1-14   *Kryon Book 3 – Alchemy of the Human Spirit* by Lee Carroll

CHAPTER 2: A 'Guide' Book to Other Dimensions

In This Chapter:

- ✧ *The Universe is Made of Energy*
- ✧ *Energy Vibration Frequency*
- ✧ *Electromagnetic Energy*
- ✧ *Electromagnetic Spectrum*
- ✧ *The Frequency of Love*
- ✧ *Love, Consciousness, the Wave of Intent and Physical Events*
- ✧ *Dimensions*
- ✧ *Space-time*
- ✧ *The Veil*
- ✧ *Communication With Other Dimensions*
- ✧ *Traveling to Other Dimensions*
- ✧ *Condensed Energy = Matter*
- ✧ *Matter Summary*
- ✧ *Spiritual Chemistry*
- ✧ *Humans Emit Light*

About this Chapter

This is intended to be a reference chapter consisting of the physics background you need to appreciate the significance of the spiritual effects described in this book. It provides in fairly simple terms the basis of understanding that non-scientists will need to make sense of some of the spiritual / physical interactions in later chapters. I was advised by my Guides to put these simple explanations here to avoid cluttering the later description of spiritual effects with details of 'high school' physics. Each section presents the essential facts about a relevant physical phenomenon expressed in the simplest form possible.

However, in addition to being a reference section, this chapter contains some amazing revelations –in particular '**The Frequency of Love**' and '**Humans Emit Light**'. I think you will find a superficial scan of this chapter quite interesting.

In later chapters of this book you will find references to the physics – and chemistry – introductory notes in this chapter. I have tried to put the items in the same order in which they come up in later chapters, but it is still quite arbitrary. I leave you to choose what you need from this scientific smorgasbord.

The Universe is Made of Energy

I believe that the energy is God or Spirit. Seth's name, 'All That Is,' seems particularly appropriate (Ref. 2-1). Part of the energy exists in forms that we recognize as energy, for example light and heat. The rest is condensed into atoms; what we humans call matter – solid, liquid or gas.

Energy Vibration Frequency

Whatever form the energy takes, it is vibrating, and the rate at which it vibrates, called frequency (Figure 2-1), determines its nature or how it manifests. For example, the energy that we call light is vibrating at a different rate than the energy condensed into atoms in matter.

It seems there are endless ways in which the energy can vibrate. A simple analogy is the vibration of a violin string when it is bowed (Figure 2-2). (In this case we hear the sound through vibration of air molecules set in motion by the vibration of the string.) The string can vibrate in the fundamental wavelength, which takes up the full length of the string. Also possible are harmonic vibrations in which several smaller wavelengths fit into the length of the string. Because wavelength is the inverse of frequency, shorter waves equal higher frequency (Figure 2-1). We perceive these harmonics as higher frequency notes. Several frequencies from the different modes of vibration of the string combine to give us the rich tone we associate with violins.

The energy of the universe has infinitely more ways of vibrating than a single violin string, so we can think of it as a vast symphony of manifested form. No wonder we humans like music, in it we perceive a reflection of the structure of the universe.

Electromagnetic Energy

Energy is free to move around in the universe and take on different forms which are interchangeable. For example, on Earth heat energy radiated from the sun heats water in the oceans so that the thermal energy transferred to the molecules makes them move faster and the water evaporates. When the condensed water vapor falls as rain or snow on mountains, it is in a high place so we say it now has potential energy. When that water is acted upon by gravity, it flows down the mountain as creeks and rivers and since it is moving it has kinetic energy. Humans have learned how to make that flowing water drive a water wheel or, in modern terms, a turbine. In this way we can convert the flow of the water into rotational energy and by using this to drive a dynamo we can generate electricity. (Analogy – think of a bicycle with a dynamo in the wheel hub to run the lights.)

We connect that electrical energy to a toaster and turn it back into heat energy to change bread into toast. As you eat your toast, did you stop to think that the energy to make it ultimately came from the sun? In fact, almost all the energy we use on this planet, with the exception of nuclear and geothermal energy, comes from the sun.

Practically all animals on this planet make use of the form of radiated energy we call light. In the nineteenth century, several scientists, such as Michael Faraday, James Clerk-Maxwell and later Albert Einstein, grappled with the question, "What is light?" Out of the mental melting pot to which these great minds contributed came the idea that electricity and magnetism were somehow connected; they worked hand in hand. Their concept was: what we call light is the result of the combined effect on our eyes of waves in electrical and magnetic fields. And these waves were mutually supporting because magnetism creates electricity and electricity creates magnetism. You can get the idea from Figure 2-3.

Electromagnetic Spectrum

There are many different forms of this electromagnetic energy. You may have wondered why it is that in a relatively short time the sun can not only warm us but also burn us, yet for hours we can sit in front of a fire, which feels as hot as the sun during the day, and we get warmed but not burned. The answer lies in the different energy content of light and heat. Although they are both electromagnetic radiations, the frequency of the light is higher than that of heat. The higher the frequency, the greater the energy – you can think of higher frequency giving more pulses of energy in a given time. So the higher frequency of ultraviolet light from the sun delivers more energy per second than the infrared heat from a fire. We humans now understand there are many forms of radiated energy, depending on its frequency, and that it includes X-rays, microwaves and radio waves, as shown in Figure 2-4.

Looking at Figure 2-4, if we start at the long wavelength end of the visible light spectrum – the red part of the rainbow – on the left we have big, relatively low energy waves that we call infrared, i.e., below red. They're the ones responsible for us feeling the heat of a fire or the sun. (They're also the ones that get trapped in the Earth's atmosphere and lead to global warming.) Our remote controllers use these waves to change our TV channel.

At longer wavelengths we have microwaves that cook our food and run our cell phones. Still longer waves carry our radio and TV programs. (By the way, abbreviations AM and FM – types of radio signal – use two of the terms connected with waves in Figure 2-1. They stand for 'amplitude modulation' and 'frequency modulation.')

Still looking at Figure 2-4 – back at red in the visible light spectrum, we can move through shorter wavelengths passing yellow, green and blue until we get to violet. (As wavelength decreases and frequency increases, we have more little waves of energy crammed into a second, Figure 2-1, giving us more frequent pulses of energy per second.   Short wavelengths equal high frequencies, which equal high energy.) When we go to just slightly shorter wavelengths than the visible violet we get into the region of ultraviolet waves which are responsible for chemical reactions in our skin like tanning and sun-burn.

At even higher frequencies we encounter X-rays which have so much energy they can penetrate our bodies and still affect a photographic film.   At frequencies beyond that, we encounter radiation from other parts of the universe. We call these cosmic rays and we think they come from stars beyond our solar system. This radiation has such high energy it can penetrate our planet.

The Frequency of Love

What follows is not part of accepted science. It comes directly from my Guides. It refers to the electromagnetic spectrum of radiation that we just considered, but at fantastically high frequencies, much higher than conventional science deals with. To give you an idea of how far out it is, I need to show you a way of representing frequencies as powers of ten. Please bear with this bit of mathematics because it will help you understand how much power our emotions have, especially love.

I expect you are familiar with the concept that 10^2 (10 X 10) is 100; 10^3 (10 X 10 X 10) is 1,000; 10^4 is 10,000 and so on. We can represent big numbers by big powers of ten. For example, I can tell you that the frequency of the microwaves that cook your food is 10^{10} hertz (hertz = cycles per second) and X-rays have a frequency around 10^{18} hertz. The most powerful radiation on Earth known to humans (i.e., scientists) is gamma radiation from radioactive materials at frequencies up to 10^{23} hertz.

But here's the big announcement about this from my Guides:

- Human emotions are transmitted in the form of electromagnetic radiation.
- The frequency of hate (=fear?) is 10^{27} !
- The frequency of love is 10^{33} !
- That means that love is 1,000,000 times more powerful than hate and 10,000,000,000 times more powerful than the most powerful radiation we humans have observed and measured on Earth.

Here is a measure of the power of love! No wonder we are told that love is the most powerful force in the universe. Kryon says that love is the basis of intent and it can overcome physics (Ref. 2-2). Love is the most powerful form of the energy that comes to us from hyper-dimensions – dimensions 5–12 - as explained in Chapter 5.

Love, Consciousness, the Wave of Intent and Physical Events

Some physicists agree that there is an effect of consciousness on physical events. It seems that Kryon's connection of love with intent is the key. In her book The Field (Ref. 2-3), Lynne McTaggert describes experiments at Princeton Engineering Anomalies Research that suggest that people and animals can influence physical events as follows:

- People were able to influence by their intent the operation and outcome of physical machines generating random events (such as thousands of balls falling down a 'pinball' frame to form a normal distribution curve). Women had a greater effect when occupied by a neutral task at the same time – i.e., multitasking. Men did better by focused concentration.
- Pairs of people did better than individuals. The pairs effect was three times greater than singles when the pairs were a male and female. And they were six times better when the couples were in a relationship. (They were resonating more!)

- Freshly hatched chicks – imprinted with a robot as a mother hen – were able to bring a random robot closer to them than expected by chance. Rabbits were able to keep a robot with a bright light – which the rabbits did not like – farther away from them than by chance. So it seems that it's consciousness – not necessarily human – that can have an effect at a distance.

Finally, there were some surprising results in this area of research when it was noticed that the random event generators were influenced by events that brought the attention of many people into one focus, for example, the O.J. Simpson trial or the death of Princess Diana. It seems that when the emotions of a large number of people are focused on some event, they emit a 'wave of intent' (Angels' words -MKS) that can be detected by the random event generators and presumably other humans and animals. Other experiments suggest this effect is the basis of remote healing.

Dimensions

Before I tackle this subject, which is quite difficult to describe, I feel I should say a few words about what is meant by the universe. In my classes I have noticed some confusion about what is meant by this term. My definition of the universe is all the physical existence that we can perceive with our five senses. That includes our planet, the solar system, the millions of stars in our galaxy – referred to in English as the Milky Way – and all the other galaxies and nebulae that our telescopes can detect.

Now back to dimensions. Usually when most people hear that word they think of measurements, for example, the dimensions of a box are its length, width and depth. This is the world of three dimensions in which we live. When we go to the movies we see a representation of three dimensions, but on a flat screen which we know to be two dimensional. However, with some cinematic processes, we can see a better simulation of three dimensions by wearing special glasses which make the scene have apparent depth by tricking our eyes and brain.

Space-time

About the time that young Albert Einstein was starting to think about relativity, humans realized that there was a fourth dimension which we know as time. For example, a bus timetable shows us four dimensions – the location of the bus in three-dimensional space relative to the time (fourth dimension) when it's supposed to be at any particular location. That makes us realize we live in a four-dimensional world and, by extension, it appears that the universe is four dimensional too. One of Einstein's contributions was that he showed time and space are knit into a four-dimensional structure which he called space-time.

We are familiar with magnets as a source of energy; a paperclip will jump off a table to a small magnet held above it. Magnets seem to have an inexhaustible energy source. If you take ten pieces of iron and magnetize them by stroking them with a magnet, they all gain magnetic energy that will attract other pieces of iron or steel to them. But the strange thing is that in spite of passing magnetic energy to the ten pieces of iron, the original magnet retains its strength. Where has that energy come from? It's not like a cell phone battery that has to be charged up every so many hours of operation. About the time Einstein was proving that there were four dimensions in our universe, a Polish scientist called Kaluza suggested that magnetism came from a fifth dimension. In fact, he wrote to Einstein about it and after some discussion they agreed that Kaluza should publish the idea (Ref. 2-4).

So now we have five dimensions! To cut a long story short, physicists have been working on the concept of dimensions ever since Einstein and Kaluza started this research, and they have now decided that the universe probably contains eleven dimensions. (If you are interested, the area to check is called 'string theory.') But of course, like so many physicists' theories, this is mostly based on mathematics and most people want to know if this has any basis in what we call reality. To give them their due, the physicists concerned said that most of these extra dimensions are probably curled up somewhere in the universe. In fact, some suggested that in the centre of every atom there were other dimensions, i.e., the 5–11th dimensions were curled up inside the four dimensions that we inhabit. This is interesting because we will see later that the Angels and Guides talk about 'going inside' our cells to access the 5th dimension where they live.

But this is difficult to imagine. Let's see what a being who is not bothered by four-dimensional constraints says about this. Kryon tells us the physicists missed a dimension in their mathematics and, in actual fact, there are twelve (I will use this number in future). But the physicists were almost right when they said the 5–11th dimensions were curled up in the universe. Kryon says those extra dimensions are more like ingredients in a cake. We know the ingredients the recipe called for, but when we cut the cake we can't point to the flour or the egg, although we know it's there when we taste it. Dimensions are like that – we can't see them but we can connect with them, our spirit can even go there, e.g., by an out-of-body trip. Kryon says once we learn to go to the 5th dimension we have a ticket to all the other seven (Ref. 2-5), so we don't have to give up our life in four dimensions to experience all the rest. However, that is what we do when we die.

Another way of looking at dimensions is by going to our original definition of matter as energy that is vibrating. Just as a violin string can vibrate at its fundamental frequency and at several harmonics, Figure 2-2, so energy can vibrate at many (infinitely many?) frequencies. At one frequency, vibrating energy is perceived as a proton, at another frequency, an electron. At a different range of frequencies we call the vibrating energy light because it affects the cellular structures we call eyes in a particular way. By the same token we can think of dimensions as being energy vibrating at twelve different frequencies. We are quite comfortable with the concept of radio and TV vibrations of electromagnetic energy being all around us. We are used to tuning our receivers to one particular frequency for our favourite channel. I suggest we spirits are used to tuning our <u>physical existence manifestations</u> that we call bodies, and all their constituent atoms, to the frequencies of the four dimensions we inhabit.

One day my Guides and I were discussing what is meant by a dimension. They suggested that the change in angle of a hand on a clock as it moves from 12 to 1 is equivalent to a dimension. That made me think that since one way of looking at dimensions is vibration of energy, then perhaps the direction of the vibration is like the angle between 1 and 12. In Figure 2-1, the height of the peak of the vibration wave is called the amplitude. The amplitude has the quality of orientation, i.e., the vibrating energy vibrates in one particular direction. What I gathered from my Guides was that the angle at which the vibration was orientated may also constitute the difference in dimension. So I suggested that what we perceive as one of the three space dimensions is the result of the orientation of the amplitude of the vibration as well as its frequency. They said:

Eggsactly, we couldn't say it better ourselves.
But they added that this directional quality applies to dimensions 1–5, the others (6–12) are curled up. Then we discussed the creation process and they said:
Each of the first four dimensions are the directions Spirit chose to have energy vibrating in.
This was to create a space in which a physical universe could be experienced.

If you would like to follow this up more then I suggest you look into Drunvalo Melchizedek's book *The Ancient Secret of the Flower of Life* (Ref. 2-6). There he explains, in terms of sacred geometry, how the creation process is thought to have proceeded. The creation of three different directions at right angles to each other is the critical first operation of this process.

The Veil

We are beginning to realize that some people – we call them medium, shaman or a whole host of names – can tune their spirit to a frequency we now call the 5th dimension, and by virtue of Kryon's 'ticket,' to all the rest of the 6–12th dimensions. It appears that what spiritualists refer to as the 'veil' is really the division between dimensions 1–4 and dimensions 5–12. (When they talk about departed humans being on 'the other side' they mean the other side of the veil.) We are also told that in recent times the veil is becoming thinner and that is facilitating communications between humans and the beings that inhabit dimensions 5–12.

To complete this picture, we can consider death as tuning our spirit back to the 5th dimension. Perhaps a better way of expressing this is to say that our spirits are tuned to the 5th dimension as a natural state, i.e., in the life between lives – where we come from when we are born and where we go back to when we die. And I believe we keep making that transition; we call it reincarnation. Birth is a process of arranging for a new body to be tuned into the four-dimensional vibrations, our spirit inhabits it for another physical experience or lesson and then we tune our spirit back to our normal state, the 5th dimension.

Communication With Other Dimensions

I was very interested to hear from my Guides how communication between dimensions works – when we channel or use the pendulum, how does our body receive the message?

Here's the mechanism broken into steps:

- The first step in understanding this comes from Kryon (Ref. 2-7). He tells us that our DNA – the heredity material in every cell of our bodies – consists not only of the two physical strands, referred to as the double helix, but also ten magnetic strands. (He backs up this information by reference to a crop formation that occurred in England in 1996.) We can think of the DNA complex as a biological computer in every cell of our bodies. The physical strands are the hardware and the magnetic strands the software.

- We saw a few pages back that Kaluza theorized that the apparently inexhaustible power of magnetism comes from the 5th dimension. That's where the Angels and Guides are and they send magnetic signals to our DNA where it's received by the magnetic strands. The signal is passed to the physical strands by electromagnetic induction – an effect that engineers use to make transformers that change electrical voltage. Scientists have shown the DNA physical strands conduct electricity so it is possible for the magnetic signal to be transferred to them as an electrical signal.
- The electrical signal is passed through our bodies, maybe by normal conduction or maybe by quantum effects which will be described in Chapter 6. It is received into our consciousness and operates certain muscle groups depending on the mode of communication. In the case of a person channeling, the muscles operate the person's voice box. Similarly, for a medium speaking a message for a dead person, the muscles operate the medium's voice box. For someone operating a pendulum or doing automatic writing, the small muscles that control hand and finger movement are activated.
- This is how the message comes from the 5th dimension into our four space-time dimensions.

Traveling to Other Dimensions

As a result of some of their research into fundamental physics, for example, as part of string theory that we touched on earlier, many scientists believe that some aspects of the 5–12th dimensions, referred to as hyper-dimensions, can be found in the interior of our four-dimensional atoms. I asked my Guides about this and they said that not only was this theory correct but it is the basis of how they take my spirit on trips to other dimensions. Here's an idea of the procedure we usually follow:

First I go into a meditation in which I usually imagine myself on a cliff overlooking the sea. My Guides then come to me in various 'fancy dress' outfits and on modes of transport related to the trip we are about to take. For example, they came dressed as nineteenth-century sailors on a sky sailing ship when we were going to visit one of my previous lives in the British navy. My Guides appear to jump into my body with shouts of joy and I, as my spirit, seem to follow them.

They said recently:

We jump into your body and slide down the cells to each nucleus.
In the nucleus we enter the DNA.
DNA acts as a portal to other dimensions; it warps space zenithly
(i.e., to a maximum degree).
I asked which cells they slide down and they said:
We mean we slide down each and every cell; we use your total body.

I asked how they enter the cells and they said it was Via the tubules. (The tubules are part of the cell structure as will be explained later in this chapter in the section: **Humans Emit Light**.) I asked if they, and I, were riding a light wave down the tubules and they said, *Bingo, you have it all.*

So then I went back to their statement about DNA warping space. I asked if this was a general way to access other dimensions. They said: *Think of twisting your space-time until a split occurs.* This statement was accompanied by a vision of a strip of wood veneer being twisted into a rope until splits occurred in the wood. So I asked if they slipped through the cracks and they said that they, and my spirit, slipped through the cracks out of our four dimensions into the 5th dimension where they normally reside.

They added at the end: *This slipping through the cracks is the opposite to Angels projecting humans into four dimensions.* The significance of this will become apparent in the next chapter.

Condensed Energy = Matter

Matter is the science name given to all material – solid, liquid or gas – that exists as atoms.

Einstein showed that a fantastic amount of energy is condensed to make the smallest amount of matter. The relationship between the amount of energy (E) that is condensed in mass (m) – think of mass as weight – is given by Einstein's famous equation:

$$E = mc^2$$

Where c is the speed of light – a very large number.

In atoms, the universal energy is vibrating in little bundles at several frequencies – some at a frequency we call protons, some at neutron frequency and some at electron frequency. (This is where Spirit manifests as the physical world, hence the subtitle of this book.) In the universe's lightest kind of atom, which we call hydrogen, there is only one proton and one electron circling around it. As we move to the next heaviest atom, helium – of party balloon fame – there are two protons and two neutrons in the central nucleus with two electrons buzzing around it like a miniature solar system. And so as more protons, neutrons and electrons are added in different types of atoms, they become heavier and we have different names for them like carbon, oxygen and iron. The material made from one kind of atom is what we call an element and we believe there are about 100 – at least that humans have found – that make up all the matter in the universe.

While most kinds of atoms can exist alone, depending on the conditions, usually they like to connect up with other atoms. When atoms of different elements combine together they form molecules. For example, if two hydrogen atoms combine with an oxygen atom we get a molecule (with a shape like Mickey Mouse's head) that we call water, or H2O. When atoms combine to form molecules, the bonds between the atoms are formed by electrons from the atoms being shared. Because the shared electrons are traveling so fast – around the speed of light – it's impossible to say where they are exactly. All we can do is define a 'cloud' in which we are likely to find the electrons. These clouds of electron probability are called orbitals. We will meet this term again in Chapter 6.

Matter Summary

What modern scientists call an element is matter consisting of one type of atom. All the atoms of an element have the same structure and consist of tiny bundles of the universal energy vibrating at different frequencies, which we call protons, neutrons or electrons. Similar or different atoms join together to form molecules. Human bodies are made of molecules.

Spiritual Chemistry

It seems to me that this process of combining atoms into molecules, which humans call chemistry, is one of Spirit's ways of manifesting Itself in the universe. Continuing the process, Spirit puts a lot of different molecules together and the result is a rock, a plant, an animal or a human. Basically, our bodies are a collection of little bundles of condensed energy.

However, I believe it takes more than a collection of molecules to make a human. When a human body is created, usually it is for occupation by another part of Spirit, vibrating at a different frequency, which we understand as a soul in a human that is alive. We say that this is the God within us. This approach suggests a point of view of the body coming first and the Spirit entering into it. Really, I am told, it's the other way around. After the incarnation is planned by the oversouls (more on those in Chapter 3 – I'll call them souls for now) of the potential human and its parents, the souls initiate the building of a vehicle and that is when the molecules are put together to make the body. The soul of the new human supervises the construction. It does this through the combined DNA of the parents, the DNA acting as a portal between dimensions. My Guides explained in the foregoing section **Traveling to Other Dimensions** how DNA warps space to create a dimension portal.

As my Guides say:

"You are not physical beings having a spiritual experience but spiritual beings having a physical experience."

Humans Emit Light

We all know that humans emit heat, if we stand close to someone we can feel the infrared radiation coming from their bodies as warmth. In this section we are going to see that humans send out radiation at several different frequencies, some being surprisingly powerful.

A few years ago, Fritz-Albert Popp, a cancer researcher, discovered that cells in the human body – and all plant and animal cells – emit light (Ref. 2-8). To prove this, he built a very sensitive detector that could detect individual photons (bundles of light energy). With such equipment he eventually showed that every square centimeter of human skin emits ten photons of light in the visible wavelength region every second. He went on to suggest this was part of a mechanism through which plant or animal cells communicate.

For me this explains something I once noticed in the darkness of a rather boring technical lecture – my hands were glowing with a faint purple light. I thought it might be light reflected from the projector so I put them in the shadow under the table at which I was seated – but they still glowed in the shadow. Now I make a connection with Popp's results as I write this book and I hear my Guides laughing.

For now I just want to emphasize that it is scientifically established that living organisms, including humans, emit light. My Guides have told me that this is the basis of people feeling they are being looked at. For example, you may have had the experience of looking at someone's hair and found that the person observed touched their hair as if they felt something there. (Apparently, according to the Guides, much of the light we beam out and receive is connected with hair follicles – not actual hair – so it doesn't matter if you are bald.) It seems that the light we emit is part of our interpersonal communication equipment.

As we have seen earlier in this chapter, light is an electromagnetic radiation; it consists of interwoven electric and magnetic fields. The visible part of the radiation – what we know as the colours of

34

the rainbow – is just a narrow band in a wide spectrum of different frequencies. It makes sense to me that if we can emit one part of the electromagnetic spectrum we may also be able to emit other parts. Probably like radio waves, the emission and reception of the different wavelengths may depend on the size of the antennae that are involved. For example, Popp showed that the photons emitted from the human skin came from tiny components of each cell called tubules which are fifteen nanometers (a nanometer = one-billionth of a meter) in diameter. Maybe the atoms that constitute the tubules are the source of very small wavelength radiation. Very small wavelength is equivalent to very high frequency – like the 10^{33} hertz love radiation we saw in an earlier section of this chapter. It would make a lot of sense that love comes from the fine structure of the spiritual quantum field (See Chapter 6).

My Guides have the last word in this chapter:

Bingo! You have made another big step of understanding.

References for Chapter 2

Ref. 2-1   *Seth Speaks* by Jane Roberts

Ref. 2-2   *Kryon Book 3 – Alchemy of the Human Spirit* by Lee
            Carroll

Ref. 2-3   *The Field* by Lynne McTaggart

Ref. 2-4   *Einstein – His Life and Universe* by Walter Isaacson

Ref. 2-5   *Kryon Book 8 – Passing the Marker* by Lee Carroll

Ref. 2-6   *The Ancient Secret of the Flower of Life Volume 1*
            by Drunvalo Melchizedek

Ref. 2-7   *Kryon Book 6 – Partnering with God* by Lee Carroll

Ref. 2-8   S. Cohen and F.A. Popp: "Biophoton emission of the
            human body."
            Journal of Photochemistry and Photobiology B 40
            (1997), 187-189.
            www.lifescientists.de/publication/pub2003-04-1.htm

CHAPTER 3: Angels and Guides

In This Chapter:

Definitions of Angels and Guides

For some people Angels and Guides are interchangeable because they are perceived as essentially the same heavenly beings. I am told that they are quite distinct and have similar yet different functions. That's what this chapter is about: their similarities, their differences and how they relate to each other.

Let's start with some definitions that were given to me by my Guides, who should be experts on this topic! They said:

You can define an Angel as any being that inhabits an inter-dimensional space but has never had a life on Earth or any other planet.

By inter-dimensional space I understand my Guides to mean the 5th and/or higher dimensions (See Chapter 2). They went on to say:

It follows from that definition that guides will not be Angels since they have had one or more lifetimes on Earth.

We can conclude from this that Guides are like Angels in that they both inhabit higher dimensions. What sets them apart is that the Guides have experienced physical life on a planet and Angels have not. But this is not the only difference; as we will see later in this chapter, Angels command much more energy or power than Guides.

In this chapter I want to pass on what I have been told about the organization in these dimensions that are 'home' for the Guides and Angels. Not only is this information interesting, but it explains some of the ways in which humans receive communications from dimensions other than our four physical dimensions. Such communications have been occurring since at least biblical times. When we understand how our Angels and Guides relate to humans, then we can make more sense of less common experiences some humans have had – for example, past life connections with famous people.

However, I have to add a word of caution here: no one on Earth knows for sure how things are in other dimensions. This is because all the words we read in books have come to us through a human. Someone once said, "God doesn't send us emails!" However pure a channel may be there is always the possibility of some distortion. For example, a person speaking Spanish will use completely different words than an English speaker in response to the same thought messages. There are similar differences within one language depending on the culture and experience of the person choosing the words. This is why there may be differences between what we are told by different combinations of sources and humans. For example, Carolyn Bowyer (Ref. 3-1) tells us there are seven Archangels and Natasha Hoffman (Ref. 3-2) tells us there are ten.

Angels in the World

The word angel comes from the Greek *angelos*, meaning a messenger. Over the whole world there are many references to beings that could be thought of as angels. Christians, Jews and Moslems all believe in angel-like beings (Ref. 3-3). Hindus have Devas and in Japanese mythology there are spiritual beings with wings. In the United States, a Lakota Indian said, "What you Christians call angels we Indians call spirits." (Ref. 3-3) A common concept is that angels travel at the speed of thought, which is probably why they are usually depicted with wings.

Historical View of Angels

In early times angels were considered to be big powerful beings. The Bible, and people who have had visions of them, tell us the angels are concerned that their appearance may frighten the people seeing them. Typically they start their pronouncements with, "BE NOT AFRAID!" The concept of angels as very powerful beings is shown by a number of artists up to the year 1600, such as El Greco.

Humans started to learn more about the physical world through experimental science starting around 1600. For example, at about that time Galileo experimented with gravity by dropping balls of different weight from the Leaning Tower of Pisa. With this newfound confidence that humans derived from experimental science, the tendency was to not heed or need the miraculous aspects of our existence, such as angels. The result was that angels represented in baroque (part of the seventeenth and eighteenth centuries) architecture and art were relegated to the chubby children with little wings that we call cherubs.

Isaac Newton, and many of the scientists that followed him, regarded the solar system, and probably the universe, as a great machine, something like a clock. This mechanization of the heavens, as Rupert Sheldrake calls it in *Physics of Angels* (Ref. 3-3), caused confusion in some generations that followed. Most Christian people in the previous generation to mine firmly believed that angels lived in Heaven, which was in the sky. This belief system ran into a brick wall when space exploration started in the 1950s. For example, one old lady I knew was devastated because the astronauts did not see angels outside their spacecraft.

The exploration of outer space, and inner space by nuclear physicists, has given us a new view of the world and heavens. I think we have been helped in this by considering in our art and science the possibility of the existence of extra-terrestrials. To me it's a relatively short step from considering beings who live on other planets to those living in other dimensions.

Angels' Existence – In Their Own Words

If they're not sitting on clouds in the sky, where are they? I'll let the Angels tell you in their own words:

"We want to tell you about our realm that we inhabit, or occupy would perhaps be a better word. There is a dimension that you refer to as 5 and another that you would call 6. We are in both of these dimensions and between them. Our name is Angel, although a few of us have been in this position forever and those are referred to as Archangels. We Angels have been many things on many planets but none of us has ever had a lifetime, or any time, living on Earth although we make many visits to your four dimensions and bring help to humans who have need of it."

"We live in a kind of mist of physical energy which is not matter but is in a state about to become matter. So you would say, from your book definitions, we are partly condensed energy. This was the state human souls were in before they came to Earth and became physical, i.e., before their energy completely condensed according to A. Einstein's equation, although that applies only to the condensation of energy on the Earth plane."

"We are in this semi-condensed form so that we are recognizable to our fellows and to some humans who can see us at certain times such as the announcement of the birth of Jesus to the shepherds. Those worthy men could see us just for the short time of the announcement. Come All Ye Faithful has been the hymn that humans have composed to commemorate that event and it gives a sense of the joy that was felt by all the people connected with that event." (Appendix 2)

40

Human Experiences of Angels

From conversations I have had, it seems that a number of people, in North America at least, are familiar with two experiences that they ascribe to Angels. People refer to them as the 'Parking Angel' and the 'Library Angel.' If you're not familiar with them, here's what people describe:

Parking Angel

You are driving to an appointment with not much time to spare. You ask your Guides, your Angel or your source for help in finding a parking spot near your appointment so you don't have to waste precious time looking for a vacant spot. My Guides are experts in this convenient art; nearly always a space becomes vacant right where I need it.

I think what is happening is that you are using the Law of Attraction (see box below) to create the outcome that you desire. By visualizing outcomes I think it's possible to change your future. For most of us, who are beginners at this, getting a parking space is an event small enough for us to be able to manifest it. I think this is a valuable experience because it shows us a way to start exercising our visualization power. When we have created a few parking places we can start to believe that we have the power to visualize greater things like a job or a relationship.

The Law of Attraction

'That which we give attention to, either wanted or unwanted, comes into our experience.'

We'll talk about this more in Chapter 7

Library Angel

This experience does not appear to be initiated by ourselves but seems to come from some other source. In my case I believe my Guides usually cause it. Typically, I am researching some topic, not necessarily spiritual, and I need some information or a picture. I go to a library and look in areas where I think there may be relevant books. Suddenly a particular book catches my eye, I pull it off the shelf and, as I do, another book near it falls to the floor. I retrieve the fallen book and find in it the very information or picture I am looking for.

In *Alien Dawn* (Ref. 3-4) Colin Wilson describes how he needed a reference on alchemy. Uncertain which book he needed, he took one off his shelf and the next book fell on the floor – open at the right page.

A variant of the Library Angel experience is even more astonishing when we are introduced to a new topic that we never knew existed but is apparently on our path. I had the following experience when I was working as a product development group leader at a commercial research centre in England. One afternoon after work I was in the public library looking at books on research and development. I pulled an interesting-looking book off the shelf and the one next to it fell on the floor. As I bent to pick it up I saw its title was *Synectics* (Ref. 3-5). Never having seen this word before, I was interested to find its meaning. So I read a little and found out it was about the practice of group creativity to invent new things. I took the book home and started to read it. Two days later, the phone in my office at work rang. Bill the Research Director asked, "Malcolm, have you ever heard of Synectics?" This collection of coincidences was laid before me and I gladly followed the path to which it led me. I became trained in Synectics technique and started a group that used these methods at the research company. Several UK Patents were awarded for the inventions that the Synectics group developed. (Synectics is discussed in greater detail in Chapter 7.)

Guardian Angel Interventions

It seems to me that there are two types of guardian Angel intervention:

- Critical help in life-or-death situations
- Assistance in following your path

I have had both kinds of experiences and will tell you about them next.

World War II Air Raid

Toward the end of the war, around 1944, the bombing attacks on Portsmouth had eased. My mother and I left our evacuation billet on a berry farm in the nearby country and returned to live in Portsmouth with my Dad. We were not to know that another, more random form of bombing was about to start. The Nazis sent pilotless ramjet-powered planes loaded with explosives. They called them vengeance weapons (V1) and we called them 'doodlebugs.' The motors were supplied with enough fuel to get the plane over the target city and then, when the fuel ran out, the plane would glide silently for a few seconds before crashing in an enormous explosion.

One night when I was eight years old I was woken up by Mum – my Dad was on duty with the ARP (Air Raid Precautions). She told me that the siren had just sounded to warn of a doodlebug attack. I quickly put on my dressing gown and followed Mum to the yard. Our plan, in the event of a raid, was to climb the five-foot-high wall to gain access to our next-door neighbours' underground shelter, which was unused at the time. We had planned to shelter there because we felt safer underground than in the surface brick shelter in our yard. We had put a wooden box against the wall to help us climb over if necessary.

The box was very necessary just then! As Mum climbed over the wall first, to where she had a better footing to haul me up and over the wall, we heard the throbbing motor of a V1 approaching. Standing on either side of the wall, we looked up and saw the flame from the V1 motor just above our neighbours' roof top. As we saw it the motor stopped and the flame went out; we knew we had about fifteen seconds before it crashed and exploded. Mum leaned over the wall shouting, "Come on Boy! – Oh please help him!", and somehow I was lifted into her arms. Still holding me in her arms, she ran the twenty yards to the shelter and threw us both down the open steps. As we hit the steps, the V1 crashed and exploded in the next street. Mum pulled herself over me as bricks from the destroyed houses rained down on us.

Lying there on the shelter steps, Mum prayed our thanks for the deliverance. She gave thanks for the man that had answered her urgent prayer and boosted me into her arms. That man was an Angel – a guardian Angel.

My Guides say:

We define guardian Angels as free agents like a fire brigade. When a human needs help his or her belief calls 911.

Hawaiian Gardener

The second kind of Angel experience is usually far from life-and-death situations. The Angel comes to you in a peaceful way with some information or something you need for your continuing journey along your life path. I believe most of the Angel incidents described in the Bible were of this kind. Here's my story:

Two of the women I worked with in the Vancouver industrial research lab, Barbara and Judy, went on a vacation in Hawaii. When they returned to work, they were full of a tale about an unusual man they had met in a Honolulu botanical garden. He had shown them around the park and told them about the plants growing there. As they left he had told them to send their friends. Barbara and Judy told me, "Malcolm you're supposed to meet him. He appeared to be

44

Japanese but he seemed really unusual. We feel he is an alien from a UFO!" (In later chapters I will talk about this apparent crossover between Angels and aliens.)

About a year later, I went to Honolulu with some of my family. I recalled my colleagues' urging to meet 'the alien.' Each morning on that vacation I considered going to the botanical gardens but each time the message was – not today! About the eighth day we were in Honolulu, I suddenly felt that was the day to go to the park, so we went there. As I paid the admission fee and turned to walk in the entrance I saw him. He was a small Japanese man and I knew immediately he was the man my friends had met the previous year. As we walked through the entrance he was saying goodbye to another young man. We passed close to him and he turned to me and said, "Welcome." He walked with us and said he would show us around the gardens, and he did for the next two hours. He had an intimate knowledge of all the Hawaiian plants and several times he pulled fruit off trees to give to my children. While they were eating some of the fruit, he took me aside and gave me two things: a small purple flower and a macadamia nut, still in its spherical shell. He told me I would need these things later. As we said goodbye, I asked his name and he told me Paul. I asked if he was employed by the gardens, he smiled and said, "No, I just come here to talk to people about the plants." I felt he was much more than he said.

Back in Vancouver I resumed my work on technical problems. Several months after the Hawaiian trip, I was in one of the company's plants working on a production problem. I was attending a meeting with a team that had been looking for a solution to this problem for some time. As we discussed the problem, someone asked a related question and I said that I had some notes on something similar in my briefcase. I reached into the lid of the briefcase, where I kept a small notebook. I had forgotten that was where I had put the flower and macadamia nut. As soon as my fingers, searching for the notebook, touched the nut, the answer to the technical problem came to me in a flash. I pulled back my fingers as if I were burned – in a way, I was burned by the power that came to me through the nut. The incident made me realize that nut was special.

At just about that time my Guides had told me through automatic writing that I should get a pendulum. I now understood what the Hawaiian garden Angel meant when he had said that I would need that nut. I drilled two holes in it on opposite side of the shell. Into one hole I glued a length of string and into the other a small nail – as a pointer. That nut became the pendulum that I have used ever since that day to 'read' the messages my Guides send me through an alphanumeric chart. And the small purple flower? That represented knowledge.

There's a postscript to this story. I was telling Marjorie, a sensitive friend, the pendulum story I have just recounted. She said, "When I needed a pendulum I received it in an unusual way too. One morning I found mine inside the daily newspaper delivered to my front door step. I guess the Angels slipped it in there!"

Two more points about these kinds of encounters:

- In emergency situations it is rare that we actually meet an Angel in human form. It seems more likely that we just experience an awareness of being helped. This was the case when I was boosted over the wall as the V1 was gliding to its crash point. All I experienced was a lifting into my mother's arms, although she saw the booster as a man and we realized afterwards that he must have been an Angel.
- In non-emergency situations, which may include a life-altering insight or gift, then it seems more common to meet an Angel in human form. Often, when warning about an upcoming event, the Angel has some attention-grabbing characteristic. One story told of an Angel who brought a warning to American soldiers in Iraq; she appeared to be an Iraqi woman but over her yashmak they saw two penetrating blue eyes.

Finally we may wonder why Angels help us like this. Is it an example of service to humans in lesson on this planet? I think it is, but it's also more than that. I think the Angels not only bring

46

physical assistance but, being messengers, they also awaken us to the greater reality of the world of Spirit. Most humans fuss and worry about trying to control their part of the physical world; they are so wrapped up in it that they have forgotten there is an unseen world of Spirit all around us. My Guides tell us that the Angels' message is:

Relax, just be and be loved by God.

Organization of Angels

There were three people in history who became known as experts on the organization of Angels in the heavens (Ref. 3-3):

- Dionysius, a Syrian monk writing in the sixth century.
- Hildegard of Bingen, a German abbess in the 1100s.
- St. Thomas Aquinas, a thirteenth-century theologian.

All three wrote about the ways in which Angels were organized. Although they differed in details, basically, these very spiritual people considered that there were about ten orders of Angels arranged in a hierarchy, meaning that some were 'higher' or more evolved than others. Since historic times, armies have been organized this way with 'orders' flowing down from a king or whoever was at the top. So for humans, it seems quite normal to be organized in their work with a boss at the top who delegates to managers who tell workers what to do. This is an example of how the culture of a person influences the information they channel.

In recent times we humans are hearing more about 'flat' organizations, i.e., hierarchies consisting of only one level. Kryon through Lee Carroll (Ref. 3-6) and Uriel through Caroline Bowyer (Ref. 3-1) are very definite about this. They both tell us that vertical organization charts are a thing of the human dimensions. No one part of the angelic realm is considered better than any other. For example, Kryon says it's a one-level hierarchy. Each part is honoured for its purpose and service.

I'll let the Angels tell you about their organization in their own words (Appendix 2):

"Now we wish to tell you that we are not organized into choirs and different ranks such as Seraphim and all the categories that humans have put us in. Instead we have specializations in purpose as you have seen in your chart of the duties of the Archangels. We Angels are connected with one of those specializations, or in some cases with two or three of them. You will see what we mean if you look at your chart that you constructed from our words given in the 'Standing Stones Speak.'" (Ref. 3-2)

"Now we tell you how we interact with humans. Some of us do not have specific humans associated with us, but those Angels in that state are in a minority. Those Angels act as messengers interacting with any humans and beings on other planets, what you would call extra-terrestrials. Those free-of-human-responsibility Angels frequently accompany UFOs that provide the crop circle energy stamps. It is part of those Angels' duties to provide energy backup for the energy stamps."

"However, the majority of Angels are associated with individual humans. And as you already know each of us is responsible for two or three humans (sometimes as many as seven) which you call aspects. In that role you humans have called us Angels oversouls and it seems to convey a good sense of meaning so we are happy to use that term."

ARCHANGEL	PLANET OR SUN	SPECIAL MISSION
Michael	Sun	- Responsible for the energy coming to Earth from Sun, for the full electromagnetic spectrum which is the activating principle of DNA. - Creating a focus for fulfillment of higher human potential, balancing male and female energy.
	Sirius	- A new pattern on the Earth parallel to Sun's pattern and bearing universal Love.
Zadkiel	Jupiter	- Helps the creative forces to flow more easily by balancing inspiration with human mental and physical activities.
Zaphkiel	Neptune	- Sustenance for human souls. This archangel and planet keep our feet on the ground while allowing us to reach to Heaven for guidance.
Raziel	Uranus	- Bring wisdom and insight to see below the surface of things and events.
Metatron	Pluto	- Empower transformation of the old into the new.
Raphael	Venus	- Help with personal healing and creative projects. - Open up unconscious areas to new awareness.
Hanael	Mars	- Bring confrontational energies. - Challenge every situation that lacks the creative element and does not cause soul growth.
Gabriel	Mercury	- Ambassador between Creator and created. - Bring spiritual knowledge behind all existence.
Samael	Saturn	- Allows us to accept limitations of earthly time. - Gives understanding of the immortality of the soul.
Sandalphon	* Earth	- Has the task of holding Spirit in matter.

* Earth, being a receptor of the vibrations from the other planets, is the prime place where the influence from all the Archangels comes together.

Our Personal Angel and Guides

So far in this chapter we have been talking about the activity and organization of Angels in a general sense. Now I want to bring it down to a personal level by asking the question, "How do we personally relate to the beings in our lives that we refer to as Angels and Guides?" You may not have reached the stage in your personal belief system where you believe in inter-dimensional beings around us. But since you are reading this book, it seems likely that you are at least curious about the presence of something 'supernatural' around us. My Guides and I want to assure you that as soon as you allow Angels and, or Guides into your belief system, maybe on a trial basis, they will make their presence felt. (That is what the poem "Forty Four" in the first chapter is about!) From everything that I have learned, I believe this experience will be beneficial.

After reading Kryon, talking with my Guides and after several years of being aware of my Angel, I have come to the conclusion that the following statement in my Guides' words is correct:

All humans have an Angel and at least two Guides available to help them.

I am now going to tell you about the relationship between the Angel and each human but the Guides will come into this because they have an agreement with the Angel. First, let's talk about the Angels and other names by which they are known:

- Golden Angel – with the same face as the human – Kryon's description (Ref. 3-7)
- Oversoul – a name from Seth/Jane Roberts (Refs. 3-8, 3-9)
- Higher self – with connections to psychology

The total energy of our Golden Angel, or oversoul, is far too great to be able to exist in a single human body. For that reason, the Angel sends several parts of itself called aspects (Ref. 3-8) into the Earth plane as humans. I am told – as we just saw in the Angel

50

communication – that up to seven aspects can be sent by each Angel. In the case of my inter-dimensional 'family,' my Golden Angel Mikael has sent three aspects into the Earth plane. My inter-dimensional 'family tree' is shown In Figure 3-1.

I, Malcolm, am one of the aspects. I am told that one aspect 'sibling' is in Scandinavia. I often see, mentally, waterfront scenes that I think are in Scandinavia, maybe Copenhagen. I think these are scenes my aspect sibling is seeing and they bleed through our common Golden Angel Mikael to me. I think I once saw this man; but I will tell you about that occasion in the next paragraph. The other aspect sibling is an Englishman who lives on the east coast of Britain. Strangely enough, although I lived in England for about thirty years, I have hardly ever been to that part of Britain – it seemed that I was not meant to go there. However, I have dreams about being there on the east coast with so much detail that I am sure I would know it if I were to visit the town where he lives. As with my other aspect sibling, I believe I see in dreams what this man is experiencing as a result of bleed through our common Golden Angel Mikael.

Kryon tells us that our Golden Angel (or oversoul, or higher self) has the same face that we have. So it follows from my scientific reasoning – that if I am like Mikael in this respect and my siblings are like Mikael, then we siblings should all be like each other. I once saw a man in a European railway station that was amazingly like me – we could have been twins. We stopped and looked at each other in surprise but then hurried away without saying anything. I felt we should not actually make contact and I think he felt the same way. I have been told that we are not supposed to meet our aspect siblings in this Earth life. But I feel sure my Scandinavian sibling and I were once given a brief look at each other. (For confirmation see Angel Communication in Appendix 2.)

This concept of Golden Angels or oversouls having several aspects on Earth is the subject of some amusing books by Jane Roberts, e.g., *The Education of Oversoul 7* (Ref. 3-9). Oversoul 7 is something of a beginner Angel and he has difficulty 'managing' all the lives of his aspects and keeping them out of trouble!

I think this organization of Golden Angels and aspects may explain the sometimes conflicting experiences we find when we do past life research. We share the experiences of our sibling aspects through our Golden Angel. For example, I am told that in a previous life I was Erasmus Darwin who lived in the latter half of the 1700s. But I have also recall of the life, and particularly death, of Antoine Lavoisier, a pioneering chemist who was guillotined during the French revolution, all of which took place in the latter half of the 1700s. When I asked my Guides about this apparent discrepancy they told me about aspects and explained that we could share the experiences of our sibling aspects.

Was it Mikael that helped me get over the garden wall to the air raid shelter in my doodlebug raid story, or was it one of the 'fire brigade' Angels my Guides talked about? I don't know. But as always in this kind of situation my Guides know. I asked them, and here's what they said:

It was a fire brigade Angel because your mother called, you did not know Mikael then.

Help From My Golden Angel

About the time that I first heard, from Kryon, about Golden Angels, I was having problems with driving on roads crowded with traffic, heavy articulated trucks in particular. I had been under a lot of stress in my technical work, I had a near-miss incident with a logging truck and, as a result of these two things, I got shingles – an infection of part of the nervous system. After that disease subsided I still suffered from the pain it caused when I was driving in fast traffic, particularly near articulated trucks. I found that my Guides were not able to help much in these situations but they gave me the name of my Golden Angel. When I had to pass a heavy articulated truck at high speed I asked Mikael for help and I found his love

52

steeled me for the task – without any shingles pain. I later found out that my Guides were not able to respond as quickly and with the same power of love. Since that time I have asked Mikael for help in other emergency situations, emotional as well as physical. He always gives me strength to pass 'the next truck'!

This is the first time in this chapter that I have mentioned the relationship between Angels and Guides. This is something that I shall be talking about later in this chapter, but I want to say a few words here about the relative amount of power available to both types of being. As we defined at the beginning of this chapter, Angels have never had experience of life on Earth or any other planet but Guides have had experience of life on Earth, i.e., they have been human at some time. It follows that they must have been aspects of an Angel at the time they were human. While human the Guides have had to share their Angel's power with aspect siblings. So the Guides now have access to power that is only a fraction of the energy the Angels have.

Our Guides

At the beginning of this chapter I gave you my Guides' definitions of Angels and Guides. To refresh your memory here they are again:

You can define an Angel as any being that inhabits an inter-dimensional space but has never had a life on Earth or any other planet.

By inter-dimensional space I understand my Guides to mean the 5th and/or higher dimensions. They went on to say:
It follows from that definition that guides will not be Angels since they have had one or more lifetimes on Earth.

On another occasion – after explaining about aspects – they added that because they have had lives on Earth they were sent there as an aspect of an oversoul:

We are not Angels but, like you, are aspects of Angels.

53

I am told we all have at least two Guides. I have sixteen and the reason I have so many is connected with my tasks of writing this book and others like it. At least every morning I communicate with them via pendulum and alphanumeric chart. Often this is done while I eat breakfast. They told me they did not mind us talking while I eat – after all, I regard them as family and mealtimes are often a time for family communication. The topics we cover are many and varied and I hope you will get an appreciation from this book of the information, explanations and advice they bring me. For this reason I will not go into a long discussion about their gifts; instead, I will let that description unfold as you see the way they have guided me to write this book.

You may be wondering, as I once did, about the number of Guides in the world. My thought was, with the vast number of humans on the Earth, are there enough Guides to allow two Guides for every human? The answer is simple and in two parts:

• Guides are shared among several humans.
• Incarnated humans act as part-time Guides for other humans.

Kryon sums it up well: "The guides are specialists in service to support us in lesson."

An Agreement between Our Personal Angel and Guides

This seems an appropriate point to talk about an agreement between Angels and Guides at the birth of each human. It seems to me that the best way to present this is in the words of my Guides. Therefore, I will give to you as I received it from my Guides on August 6, 2008:

In this instance we have told you before about an agreement between Angels and Guides.
Usually the starting Guides and the oversoul (of the new human) *meet with the parents' oversouls.*
This is done as the act of insemination occurs.
This leads to DNA from the father and the mother combining.
The combined DNA creates a portal (in the veil – see Chapter 2 for description of this effect) *through which the oversoul injects a*

template.

The template conveys the information to the forming molecules.

The template conveys not only physical data but also personality and karma (i.e., life plan) – *stuff which accompanies aspects of souls as they incarnate.*

At this occasion the guides form an agreement with the Angel oversoul.

It is an agreement of devotion.

The template – injected into the Earth plane by the oversoul – as described by my Guides appears to be the same thing as the morphic field suggested by Rupert Sheldrake (Ref. 3-10). Sheldrake describes it as an energy field around all living things – plants and as well as animals – which directs the molecules to form cells and the cells to form a complete organism, whether it be a willow tree or a human.

The Relationship Between Our Personal Angel and Guides

As we saw above there is an agreement of devotion between the Golden Angel or oversoul and the Guides for any particular human. But we must not forget that the Guides, having been incarnated at some time, are an aspect of an Angel. This means that there is a great difference in power – love power – that an Angel and the Guides can summon.

In one of his parables, "Wo and the Rooms of Lesson" (Ref. 3-7), Kryon talks about each human having a golden room into which only he/she can go – in that room is the human's 'piece of God,' or Golden Angel with his/her face. The Guides are not allowed to enter that room. I understand it is because the Guides could not withstand the great love power that is held by the Golden Angel. Only aspects of that oversoul can enter the room and share some of the great power that is held by their Golden Angel.

(If you wish to read a wonderful story about a journeying human's encounters with different Angels and eventually with his Golden

Angel, I recommend Kryon's parable: "The Journey Home". [Ref. 3-11])

A few months ago I was presented with a perfect physical demonstration of an analogy of the relationship between the inter-dimensional beings that each of us has to help us with our lesson here on Earth. I was in a very windy part of Vancouver, close to the sea shore. There was a flat area and, on this, two young men were operating kite carts – four-wheel carts with no power except that transmitted through a rope attached to a kite sailing about seventy feet above the cart. I asked my artist friend and co-researcher Michelle DeMello, who was with me on that occasion, to photograph this perfect illustration of the analogy. Figure 3-2 is the result. The kite represents the Angel – high above the human yet providing power to move him along his path. The wheels of the cart are the Guides, very much in contact with the ground and steering the human along his path in life.

References for Chapter 3

Ref. 3-1   *Angels of The First Heaven* by Carolyn Bowyer
Ref. 3-2   *The Standing Stones Speak* by Natasha Hoffman with Hamilton Hill
Ref. 3-3   *The Physics of Angels* by Matthew Fox & Rupert Sheldrake
Ref. 3-4   *Alien Dawn* by Colin Wilson
Ref. 3-5   *Synectics* by William J.J. Gordon
Ref. 3-6   *Kryon Book 3 – Alchemy of The Human Spirit* by Lee Carroll
Ref. 3-7   *Kryon Book 6 – Partnering with God* by Lee Carroll
Ref. 3-8   *Adventures in Consciousness* by Jane Roberts
Ref. 3-9   *The Education of Oversoul 7* by Jane Roberts
Ref. 3-10   *The Presence of the Past: Morphic Resonance and the Habits of Nature* by Rupert Sheldrake
Ref. 3-11   *Kryon Book 5 – The Journey Home* by Lee Carroll

CHAPTER 4: Rings of Light

In this chapter:

In the past decade an apparently new phenomenon has entered human consciousness: the occurrence of circles of light, usually called orbs. They are most often seen in photographs taken by digital cameras, for example, Figure 4-1, although some film cameras have recorded them. In fact, the rising occurrence of orbs seems to parallel the popularization of digital cameras. Some technical reasons for the confluence of orbs and digital cameras have been suggested and for an excellent discussion of the technicalities ¬ with lots of pictures ¬ I refer you to "The Orb Project" by Miceal Ledwith & Klaus Heinemann (Ref. 4-1).

Orbs – Vehicles of Angels and Human Spirits?

As these authors suggest, it seems these orbs are some form of energy since they give off light. However, in most cases, this light is not seen by anyone's eyes until the scene has been recorded by the camera. It seems that direct viewing of orbs is only possible

59

by some sensitive people, e.g., people who see auras. In addition, it has been noticed in series of several photos that an orb may not appear until the third or fourth shot, which leads to the suggestion that one or more camera flashes are necessary to 'pump up' the energy level in the orb so that it gives off light of its own that can be recorded.

The next question that needs to be answered is: "What kind of energy?" My son Adam has had an orb float into his bedroom at night. He watched it float for a while and it sent him some energy which felt electrical. When it finished, it disappeared with an electrical sounding 'pop.' This fits in well with what physicist Klaus Heinmann says in (Ref. 4-1). He says orbs have characteristics of plasma – a plasma is a gas in which all the atoms are at such high energy that they have lost electrons and become fully ionized, i.e., they are all electrically charged particles. The most familiar examples of plasma in our physical world are electrical sparks and lightning strikes. In Chapter 8, I describe my first encounter with an orb – it occurred during a thunderstorm.

Another suggestion is that the balls of light are concentrated consciousness, which may be a form of plasma we have not encountered on Earth in free form – all our familiar consciousness seems to be tied up with animate forms. This ties in well with quotes from my Guides, which the Angels summarized as follows:

Consciousness is energy aware of itself.

In (Ref. 4-1), Klaus Heinemann describes an experience with a man who – at will – could concentrate some of his consciousness or energy into a ball of light that appeared in a digital photo as an orb, located at the side of his head.

When humans go out of body, what does their spirit look like to other humans? I know from personal experience that sensitive humans can detect human consciousness that is out of body, so maybe out-of-body humans appear like a ball of light that we would call an orb. Evidence of this comes from Charles Berlitz's book of strange phenomena (Ref. 4-2). A man called Blue Haray claimed the power of leaving his body at will. This claim was put to the test at the Psychical Research Foundation in Durham, North Carolina. On one of his out-of-body trips he visited a doctor – who was not expecting such a visit. The doctor reported seeing a "red orb" flash across his room at 3:15 AM, exactly the same time Haray said he had been there.

However, orb photographs are becoming so common that not all can be explained as out-of-body humans. In some digital photographs of crowds (Ref. 4-3) there are hundreds of orbs. In (Ref. 4-1), both authors suggest that the orbs are from other dimensions of existence; most likely the 5th and 6th dimensions. (The channeled Angel communication in Appendix 2 states that Angels occupy realms that humans would call the 5th and 6th dimensions.) The reference authors suggest that orbs want to communicate with humans; they seem to exhibit unconditional benevolence for us. The orbs are often seen around people in spiritual ceremonies and in places where people are joyful, especially with music. As an example of this, Figure 4-2 shows Beth Wallace and me when we were singing and dancing. A spherical orb is visible at the side of her head. My orb is heart shaped and located near my heart.

This brief introduction to orbs suggests two possible co-existing origins:

- They are manifestations of human consciousness particularly when it is out of body.
- They may be acting as 'windows' in the veil between our four-dimensional physical existence and the higher dimensions. It appears that through these 'windows' the Angels send messages to humans. In a similar way, the 'windows' can be used as probes by which the Angels observe their aspects (see Chapter 3 for definition of this term) in action on the Earth plane.

We will see examples of the second category of orb activities in the sections below, but first I want to tell you that humans are not the only ones experiencing orbs!

Dolphin Orbs

There is evidence (Refs. 4-4, 4-5) that among extra-terrestrials (ETs) that have come to this planet in the distant past were creatures we would recognize as dolphins. The Dogon people of Mali in Africa have in their historical myth a story of a UFO landing near their settlement. The dolphin-like creatures in the UFO first formed a small pool of water and then jumped into it where they stayed while on Earth. From this pool they spoke to the Dogon people and told them of their home planet in the star system we call Sirius. They gave detailed information about Sirius – that it is a twin star and the two stars rotate around each other. The Dogon were given the relative paths of the two stars. All this information the Dogon drew on the walls of nearby caves over 700 years ago and always appointed one of their people to be guardian of this sacred information. It wasn't until 1862 that human astronomers discovered that Sirius was a double star and much later, around 1970, that the relative path of the two Sirius stars were calculated and shown to be identical to the Dogon cave drawing.

Further research (Ref. 4-4) has shown that this dolphin story is not confined to the Dogon in Africa. The Uros people in Peru have a similar story of dolphin-like creatures arriving in a UFO and living in Lake Titicaca from where they educated the local people. In addition, there are other cultures in the world that have a similar story.

It appears from these prehistoric myths that dolphins in our world may have their origins in interplanetary traveling cousins on other planets. There is no doubt from human experiences with dolphins, and most cetaceans, that they are extremely intelligent, sentient beings. Kryon tells us they are sacred and, together with the whales, they will lead humans to knowledge in the future (Ref. 4-6).

In spite of the above information tucked away in the back of my mind, I was surprised when my Guides told me that dolphins have orbs in their world too. A friend had sent me a video clip of dolphins playing with ring-shaped bubbles. It seemed peculiar that the bubble rings were so stable and they stayed intact and vertical until the dolphins 'bit' a part out to make a smaller ring or collapsed the whole ring in their mouths. In other scenes of this video, a dolphin playfully swam through a ring which expanded to accommodate the dolphin.

Puzzled by the stability of the ring bubbles, I asked my Guides. Here's the answer they gave:

Dolphins create the rings by piping air into an orb.
Humans cannot see the orbs but the dolphins can.
As the dolphins play they are communicating with their higher self Angel.
Many people have seen this behavior but do not connect it with orbs.
Before humans came to Earth dolphins were doing this.

Orbs Bearing Messages and Acting as Probes

While the proliferation of orb experiences in digital photos is new, the occurrence of rings of light is not. They have served to mark certain humans as special. The message of the halos was that the bearers were 'holy.'

The *Encyclopedia Britannica* tells us that in Greek and Roman art the sun gods were represented with a crown of light rays. The halo was adopted by Christian Roman emperors for their official portraits but it wasn't until the fourth century that Christ was depicted with this imperial attribute. Since those times, it has been the custom to represent in works of art persons considered to be holy with a ring of light around their head. It was generally accepted that halos were seen around the holy one's head by devout observers and so the convention was used by the artist to emphasize the holiness.

Miraculous Events

Eyewitness accounts tell us that a fairly frequent feature of miraculous events is the appearance of balls of light – I shall continue to refer to them as orbs – at some time during the miracle, often preceding it. For example, one well-publicized event (Ref. 4-7) was the miracle of Fatima:

In Portugal during 1917, three children were minding goats when a vision of a lady appeared over a little oak tree near them. The children were told by the lady, whom they assumed was the Virgin Mary, to return to the same location on the thirteenth of each of the following months. As directed, on the thirteenth of the following five months, the children returned to the Cova da Iria – the little glade where the vision first appeared – and each time saw, or heard, the lady. Each time they returned they brought members of their families and people from the village. The fame of the appearances grew so that by the sixth and last occasion there were thousands of people present, including newspaper reporters that recorded the events.

On that last occasion, as in the previous ones, the first thing that happened was that an orb – also reported as a little bright white cloud – came from the distance over the tree tops and settled on the top branches of the little oak tree. It was in the ball of light that the vision of the lady was seen by at least the children, although some of the adults claimed they could also see it. Most of the people could not see the orb although some reported seeing the top branches of the little oak tree being weighed down as if something were resting on them.

(According to several witnesses, after the orb left the scene the branches of the little tree remained bent down for several hours. As we will see later in this chapter, this effect is similar to wheat stalks remaining bent after the formation of a crop circle. The Fatima witnesses also reported hearing buzzing sounds coming from the tree. Similar sounds have been reported in some crop circles [See Chapter 8].)

64

Also, on that last occasion witnessed by thousands of people, there were many other miraculous events:

- It rained heavily yet, when the rain stopped, everyone's clothes were dry.
- There was a 'blizzard' of rose petals that melted as they touched the people and the ground.
- The disk of the 'sun' came down through the clouds, rotated, gave off many rays of coloured light and then went back above the clouds.

To the people of that time it seemed that the disk was the sun. However, an elementary knowledge of the actual size of the sun precludes that explanation. From the description of the sun's gyrations and light display recorded by witnesses at the site of the events and by people who watched from several kilometers away, it seems the sun was imitated by a flying disk.

Angels and Extra-Terrestrials Cooperate

To modern students of these events it seems that a likely explanation that fits the facts was that the miracle was 'stage managed' by ETs. This is not surprising since there are several other miraculous events on record (Ref. 4-7) that seem to be staged by ETs. There are also reports of events involving ETs (Ref. 4-8) that appear to have a strong religious element. So we are led to one possible conclusion that ETs and Angels, both having access to or coming from dimensions numbered five and above, are working together to 'educate' humans about their spiritual heritage and place in the universe.

My Guides say:

Zenith cooperation between all non-humans.
Nordics are mistaken for Angels.
Herald duties of Angels are often performed by Nordics.

(Author's note: Nordics are the tall, blonde ETs that have been associated with numerous UFO 'contacts' [Ref. 4-9]. They are often associated with educational and religious themes. I have memories of being educated by Nordics during childhood 'dreams'.)

We will see more evidence of this when we look at the crop circle phenomenon.

Some other miraculous events that involved balls of light as part of the phenomena are reported in (Ref. 4-7) as follows:

- In 1905 many people in north Wales participated in a religious revival. Many balls of light were seen dashing about in the sky.
- In Zaitoun, Egypt, balls of light – some in the shape of birds – were seen hovering over a Coptic church. They were followed by a glowing figure of a woman that appeared above the church on many occasions in 1950.
- In Ireland in 1879, just before the miraculous appearance of a religious tableau on the gable end of the church of Knock, a golden orb of light was seen hovering around the church.

These events suggest that the orbs that were 'vehicles' for miraculous appearances of religious figures are tools of the Angels and ETs. They are like inter-dimensional mandalas – circular religious diagrams used in Christian, Hindu and other religious devotions. We can think of these inter-dimensional mandalas as windows in the veil that separates our four dimensions from dimensions 5 and 6. (In some respects mandalas serve the same purpose as icons which in Russian orthodox churches are placed like windows on the iconostasis – a screen between the priests and the people representing the veil between Heaven and Earth.) Through these windows Angels can watch what their aspects (see last chapter for this meaning of aspects) are doing on Earth. And these windows can be used to bring us information about our spiritual heritage. My Guides confirm this, they say:

"The orbs are three dimensional mandalas.
They are sent out into the physical world as observers by Angels.
Angels are recording activities of their aspects."

Foo Fighters

No, this is not just the name of a recent rock group. The version I am talking about occurred mostly in 1944–5, long before the rock musicians were born. During the last years of World War II balls of light were frequently seen zooming around and keeping pace with Allied planes during missions over enemy territory. The lights would show up suddenly and then fly parallel with the aircraft for miles in spite of evasive action by the planes. At times, the lights flashed on and off and emitted colours such as red, orange and gold. The allied pilots called them foo fighters – a name derived from French feu for fire via an American cartoon. The natural reaction of the allied pilots was to think that these were a German secret weapon and a photographic record was kept. But after the war, when pilots from both sides got together, they found that the Germans saw them too and thought they were an Allied secret weapon.

Similar lights were seen around military planes in the Pacific theatre of operations of World War II. In the subsequent military actions in Korea and Vietnam, pilots also reported having been accompanied by balls of light. (Refs. 4-10, 4-11)

We should not be surprised that the foo fighters were generally regarded as UFOs – they really were unidentified flying objects. But in the light of the world-wide thinking about UFOs in the fifties and subsequent years, I think the foo fighters would have been regarded as interplanetary sourced phenomena.

Now in the light of the occurrence of orbs in our digital photographs, we can extend our thinking about the inter-dimensional source of orbs back to re-evaluate the foo fighters. It seems a more likely explanation that Angels beyond the veil were sending these energy probes to watch their aspects, who were flying the war planes, as they went through the test of combat.

My Guides also confirmed that the foo fighters were orbs.

Based on the wider occurrence of orb-like phenomena – wider in type and time as we have already seen, and we will see more below – we can generalize their purposes to include:

- Conveyers of information from the 5th and 6th dimensions sent by Angels assisted in some cases by ETs.
- Information-gathering probes sent by Angels to record the activities of their aspects.

Orbs as Carriers of Energy Stamps

Now I want to review some other phenomena in which orbs not only act as information carriers – either to or from the 5th and 6th dimensions – but also carry 'energy stamps'. This is a term introduced by Kryon (Ref. 4-12) to describe a template of energy which is superimposed on a receptive material – such as a growing crop – to create a design or diagram which is recognizable by humans. The concept is familiar to us as rubber stamps carrying an inked design that can be imposed on paper or some other receptive substrate. Of course, the most obvious application of this term is in the worldwide phenomenon of crop formations. But I have been told by my Guides that this is also an explanation for what they call 'spiritual printing,' which I will describe later.

Crop Circles and Similar Formations

The crop circle phenomenon appears to have been with us for many years. In England there are reports of apparently similar effects going back at least 200 years. The modern spate of crop formations started around 1980 as circles and later evolved into quite complex designs.

In the early days of the phenomenon a number of the circles were later shown to be fakes – made by various groups of people with simple tools such as boards tied to their feet. An early result of the 'faked circles confessions' was to have most people believe that all the circles were faked and this seemed to reassure many, at least in

England, that all was well and nothing supernatural was happening in their fields. However, their relief was short lived when it became apparent that people who studied these effects could readily detect differences between faked and real circles. One of the most obvious differences between faked and genuine crop formations is that the crop stalks are broken in the former and bent – but still growing – in the latter. Microscopic studies of the bent stalks from genuine formations showed that the cellular structure of the plants had been altered by some treatment that was similar to cooking in a microwave oven. As if to add emphasis to the microscopic structure results, the designs became more and more complex, occupied significantly larger areas and, in a few cases, were shown to have been formed very rapidly. These new effects ruled out their construction by humans with boards on their feet.

The occurrence of crop designs in other countries such as Germany, Japan, Canada and the United States brought the realization that this was a worldwide event. Reports later came in of circles and designs occurring in other materials such as ice on lakes, dried lake beds and river estuary mud (Ref. 4-13). It appeared that 'someone' was trying to get the attention of humans. It was probably only natural that people began to think that this was another phenomenon connected with UFOs. In fact, in England, as well as other countries, a number of UFO sightings were associated with the appearance of crop formations. So the conclusion that surfaced was that ETs had a message for us.

There have been a number of 'interpretations' of crop designs as messages about a changing energy coming to the earth. For example, in Robert Nichol's film *Star Dreams* (Ref. 4-14) one of the interpreters, Mr. Michael Glickman, says, "we are in the middle of a dimensional shift, a frequency shift, a density shift, a vibrational shift, which is shifting us from our current hard, mechanical Newtonian reality of solid objects and linear time to a fifth dimensional reality within which both time and matter crumble away to that which is more accessible to, and manipulable by, consciousness."

One of the details of formation of crop designs was the frequent sighting in the immediate area of balls of light – sometimes single balls and sometimes in groups of up to seven. The balls of light were often red, orange, green or purple – similar in some respects to the foo fighters. The idea developed that the balls of light were part of the crop design formation process. This was reinforced by many eye witness accounts of balls of light being present near crop designs. Balls of light have been filmed by a number of reliable witnesses, including professional film crews.

Frequently the balls of light and bent stalks in crop formations are accompanied by sounds such as high-frequency trilling or buzzing. (Chapter 8 describes how I experienced similar sounds in a crop formation as a ball of light downloaded a message to my spirit. Compare also these details with some details of the Fatima miracle – orbs, bent tree branches and buzzing – highlighted in the earlier section.)

There are a number of electromagnetic effects detected by the circle researchers and their equipment. This fits very neatly with the suggestion that the orbs consist of plasma – a high energy soup of ionized atoms. This mechanism is likely to be the cause of bioelectromagnetic fields in the formations. Similar fields have been experienced in stone rings and ancient earthworks so it seems not accidental that the formations are often placed close to ancient sites and often have some indigenous cultural significance. Frequently psychic effects are experienced by people during or after visits to crop formations or stone circles. Healings have been reported (Ref. 4-13), which brings us back to the spiritual component mentioned earlier in this chapter. The bioelectric fields have also been associated with changes in human DNA – part of the human consciousness evolution referred to above and emphasized by Kryon (Ref. 4-6).

Angels and Extra-Terrestrials Cooperate

In addition to the ETs having a message for us, the occurrence of orbs near the circles suggests an Angel involvement. The convergence of thinking about Angels and ETs in relation to crop circles is explained by the following from an Angel communication in Appendix 2:

"Now we tell you how we interact with humans. Some of us do not have specific humans associated with us, but those Angels in that state are in a minority. Those Angels act as messengers interacting with any humans and beings on other planets, what you would call extra-terrestrials. Those free-of-human-responsibility Angels frequently accompany UFOs that provide the crop circle energy stamps. It is part of those Angels' duties to provide energy backup for the energy stamps."

Human Emotions Resonate With Energy Stamps

So now we return to the theme of this chapter – that balls of light (I have chosen to call them orbs) are devices that are sent into our four dimensions from higher dimensions on the other side of the veil, either with messages for us or as probes to gather information. This seems to fit the description of orbs conveying the energy template of many of the designs stamped into crops and other materials. While not all the designs may come from Angels in the 5th and 6th dimensions – some may be from certain ET groups, cooperating with Angels – many of the designs appear to bring messages about the spiritual development of humans. The messages are believed to be encoded in the geometry of the designs. In this form the energy seems comparable with that of mandalas, labyrinths or even gothic cathedrals. Energy in that form, rather than words, appeals directly to our emotions like the energy of a beautiful piece of music. This unconscious acceptance of the message seems to be part of the crop formation experience. In most cases, the crop designs are complex and obscure, but the sacred geometry aspects of them are emotional like music and carry the message straight to our hearts.

My Guides say:

The designs are transmitted to your four dimensions as three-dimensional energy stamps.

71

The energy stamps are seen by humans as orbs.
When three-dimensional energy stamps impinge on surfaces they form images.
The images are seen as crop circles or as miraculous pictures on many different surfaces.
That is why balls of light are often seen over crop circles.

What they are telling me is that one function of the orbs is to bring energy templates for stamping designs into crops, ice and other natural moldable materials. But what about the situation where there is no moldable material? Then it seems the orb energy templates not only create the design but also manifest the pigments that are necessary to make the design visible. This is the basis of my Guides' allusion to miraculous pictures in the last paragraph. The next section explains how that works.

Spiritual Printing

In addition to the miraculous appearances of apparently three-dimensional religious figures like the Lady of Fatima, there have been a number of flat images that appeared miraculously on a number of substrates, e.g., textiles, plaster and stone, in many countries and in many diverse places. The images have been varied; most often a face, but also there have been figures, scenes or emblems. Close examination shows them to be made up of dots consisting of black or coloured materials on or in the surface of the substrate. In historical times most of the images were in churches. But in recent times, maybe since the advent of media coverage, there have been a growing number of image miracles not only in churches but in secular buildings and private homes.

Medieval tradition tells us the first of these images was on Veronica's veil. Veronica was a woman who lived in Jerusalem. One day, on hearing a crowd of people shouting in the street outside her house, she went to see what was happening. She saw Jesus on the road to Calvary being whipped by Roman soldiers. She struggled to the front of the crowd and wiped Jesus' face clean of blood and sweat with her veil. Afterwards, she found that a perfect likeness of Jesus had been imprinted on her veil. During medieval times several alleged 'Veronica's veils' were exhibited in European churches (Ref. 4-7).

The most famous miraculous image, which is accepted by the Roman Catholic Church as historical fact, is that of Our Lady of Guadalupe. It appeared on a Mexican peasant's cloak in 1531, just ten years after Cortes cruelly conquered the Aztec nation, when Mexico was still in political turmoil. As an example of how this kind of miracle occurs I will briefly retell, from (Ref. 4-7), the story of our Lady of Guadalupe.

Juan Diego was a native Indian who had recently taken a Spanish name as a result of adopting Christianity. In accordance with his newfound faith, he would walk several kilometers every day to church from his home village which was just north of present day Mexico City. His walk took him past a little hill called Tepeyacac and, one day, as he was passing it, he heard sweet music coming from the top of the hill. The music stopped and his name was called, so he climbed the hill and was confronted by a radiant apparition. The female figure was dark skinned like Juan and addressed him in his native dialect. She told him that she was the Virgin Mary and asked him to tell the Spanish bishop of Mexico, Fra Zumarraga, a supporter of native rights, that she wished him to build a church in her honor on Tepayacac. Awe-stricken, Juan agreed and set off immediately for Mexico City to see the bishop.

After a long wait, Juan met Zumarraga, who listened to him politely, but it was apparent to Juan that the bishop was not really convinced. Zumarraga suggested they meet again sometime to discuss at length the request for the building of a church. Juan was disappointed when he left the city so he went directly to Tepayacac, where he found the apparition waiting for him. She urged him to petition the bishop once again, so the next day Juan walked to Mexico City and told Zumarraga the story once again. This time the bishop was a little more interested and told Juan to ask for a sign of the apparition's divine nature. Juan walked back to Tepayacac for the third time and passed the bishop's request to her. She agreed and told Juan to meet her on the hill the following day.

The next day Juan was asked by the apparition to climb to the top of the little hill. There at the crest he found a wonderful garden full of flowers that he had never seen before in Mexico. The apparition picked a bunch of flowers and asked Juan to carry them to the bishop as a sign wrapped in the rough cloak that he had tied around his neck. She warned him not to open the cloak again until in the presence of the bishop.

Juan walked back to Mexico City with the flowers wrapped in his cloak. After another long wait he finally met Zumarraga and threw open his cloak to let the flowers fall to the ground. But the cloak held a greater treasure than flowers. Impressed on the inside of the cloak was a full colour image of the Virgin Mary. It was apparent that the image was not painted on the cloak but was somehow impressed into the cactus fibers from which the cloak was made. On seeing the image, Zumarraga fell to his knees in reverence, begged forgiveness for doubting the apparition and vowed to have a church built on Tepayacac as requested.

A church was built there and named for Santa Maria de Guadalupe, as requested by the apparition. The rough cloak with the wondrous image of the Virgin Mary on it was exhibited in the church. The image shows a dark-skinned maiden in prayer standing on a crescent moon supported by an Angel. In the early 1700s the original church became dangerous due to its foundations sinking and so a new basilica was built nearby and the cloak, with its precious image, was transferred into the new church.

The cloak is still there today. Although it is over 400 years old and has been exposed to incense and the heat of candles, the colours of the image have not faded. The cloak has not rotted, even though cactus fibers usually last for only 20 years it is as strong as it was the first day. Scientists from around the world who have been allowed to examine the cloak and its image say that the image does not appear to have been painted on the cloak. One part of the cloak had been torn and repaired before the miracle but the image appears to have been stamped right over the repair.

This is an example of what my Guides call 'spiritual printing.' They say:

This is an example of Angel energy being converted into matter. The formation of the coloured material resulted from an energy stamp.

My Grandfather's Image

Not all the examples of spiritual printing are portraits of religious figures. Many that have appeared in relatively recent times have been manifestations of secular figures, often familiar to the persons perceiving the spiritual print. For example, there was the well-known case of a miraculous portrait of Dean Liddel, which gradually formed on the wall of Oxford's Christchurch Cathedral between 1921 and 1923. Liddel, who was dean of the cathedral for many years, had died in 1898 (Ref. 4-7).

I would like to show you an example of spiritual printing of a head that was very familiar to me. When I was a small child living in Portsmouth, England, just before the second World War, my paternal grandfather lived with us until he died in 1941. Those were happy times for me because every day my grandfather – 'Granfer,' as I called him – would take me into Milton Park, which was just across the street from where we lived. Granfer used to tell me that he was the one that made the flowers in the park grow so well – as he often picked one for his buttonhole. As a little kid I didn't understand what he meant, but as I grew into my curious years, after Granfer had died, I asked my father about it. Dad explained that Granfer was the farmer who had cultivated all the land now occupied by the park. In fact, the big building near the centre of the park was the barn where Granfer had kept all his equipment. I knew that building well because during the war it was turned into a state subsidized restaurant where I often met my parents for lunch – my school was on the other side of the park from our home.

After I came to live in Canada in 1974 I went back to Portsmouth a few times and visited the park and the old home area, but I never bothered with photographs. In 2008, I returned to Portsmouth for a reunion with old school friends. On this visit I was led to go back to photograph the park and barn – I remember feeling it was somehow connected with this book which I had then started writing. Imagine my surprise when, back home, my Guides led me to find in the photos a white shape on Granfer's barn door, Figure 4-3. I feel that Granfer's Golden Angel was communicating with me by showing a shape that I would recognize as Granfer. I believe that shape was 'planted' there by an Angel-generated template which we would have perceived as an orb.

I didn't realize the image was there in the photo until my Guides drew my attention to it. Their words about it were:

Examine all photos from England carefully.
Granfer is showing his Angel for you.
The shape he copies from his oversoul.

The Mechanism of Spiritual Printing

It appears that the process is akin to the formation of designs in crops, ice and mud. But in the case of spiritual printing there is no moldable material to be 'stamped' with the design. Instead, the incredible energy of the Angels is condensed into physical material that we perceive as pigment particles absorbed on or embedded in the surface of the substrate. In the case of the design on the cloak of Guadalupe, the coloured pigments were embedded in the surface of the cactus fibers from which the cloak was made.

(I think it is quite likely that a similar process was involved in the creation of the image on the Shroud of Turin.)

76

How does the material of the pigments become manifest in our world? In the Angel Communication at the end of the last chapter we were told that the Angels live in "a kind of mist of physical energy which is not matter but is in a state about to become matter." The Angels tell us that according to our definitions we would call this partly condensed energy. It seems to me that this is the energy of the orbs, which we experience as ionic plasma – familiar to humans as an electrical spark. (Maybe it's just coincidental [!] but when he painted the Sistine Chapel ceiling, Michelangelo was inspired to paint the hand of God transferring a spark to the hand of man.) When it is necessary for that energy to manifest as matter – like the pigments of spiritual printing – then the energy condenses completely.

In (Ref. 4-15) Susan Rennison shows evidence that much of the energy in the universe, which we see as galaxies and supernovae, is composed of ionic plasma. Scientists tell us that in this form, the energy can be manipulated into three-dimensional forms by the application of electric and magnetic fields. It seems entirely appropriate that the power of the Angels is at the incredible magnitude involved in the structure of the universe. I am told we are seeing on a very small scale ("as above – so below") the same condensation of energy, which probably proceeds according to Einstein's equation $E = mc^2$ (see Chapter 2 for explanation). In this case, the energy condenses to form pigments on various surfaces giving us examples of spiritual printing.

I didn't realize the significance of all this until my Guides explained it as follows:

The cloak of our Lady of Guadalupe is an example of Angel energy being converted into matter.
Formation of coloured matter results from an energy stamp.
It is simply condensation of energy into matter.
This is where the spiritual chemistry takes place.
When energy condenses it does so in spirals.

(See Chapter 7 for the significance of spirals.)

The Message of the Orbs

Figure 4-4 is a photo of three birds flying toward a sunset, but the configuration of the birds immediately strikes humans, at least in the Western world, as a smiley face. I believe this is an example of natural materials being arranged 'coincidentally' into a configuration that has meaning for humans. It's just like millions of wheat stalks being bent into a geometric design visible from miles away.

I believe these are all examples of message templates superimposing an 'energy stamp' – as Kryon calls crop designs – on everyday materials, just as a painter puts coloured materials on a surface in an arrangement that is perceived as significant by humans. It seems these message templates are coming into our four-dimensional world from sentient beings in the 5th dimension.

Why are these things coming into our world just in the last 100 years? It seems to me that in spite of 2,000 years of religious experience – or maybe because of it – humans are mostly wrapped up in physical things. There are a number of spiritual people in all societies. However, in the Western world, by far the majority are engrossed in money, power, sex, sport and possession of physical things to the exclusion of all consideration of a spiritual existence. Yet we humans all came from a spiritual existence and will return back there at our death. It seems to me that our attention in schoolhouse Earth is mostly focused on the furniture and not on our lessons.

Since the 1980s we are told, e.g., by Kryon, that a new energy is coming to Earth and through it we can 'graduate' spiritually. All these orb-related phenomena, including religious experiences, miracles, crop designs and spiritual printing, look like a combined operation of all the Angels, Guides and other sentient beings beyond the veil. It seems they are contacting us to pour understanding of our true existence into as many humans as possible, and the orbs are one of their tools for delivering that understanding.

78

References for Chapter 4

Ref. 4-1	*The Orb Project* by Miceal Ledwith and Klaus Heinmann
Ref. 4-2	*Charles Berlitz's World of Strange Phenomena*
Ref. 4-3	*The Hyper-Dimensional Election of Barack Obama and 2012*, DVD by Richard Hoagland
Ref. 4-4	*The Ancient Secret of the Flower of Life – Volume 1* by Drunvalo Melchizidek
Ref. 4-5	*The Sirius Mystery* by Robert K.G. Temple
Ref. 4-6	*Kryon Book 7 – Letters from Home* by Lee Carroll
Ref. 4-7	*Miracles – A Parascientific Inquiry into Wondrous Phenomena* by D. Scott Rogo
Ref. 4-8	*The Andreasson Affair* by Raymond E. Fowler
Ref. 4-9	*Alien Dawn* by Colin Wilson
Ref. 4-10	*U.F.O. Evaluating the Evidence* by Bill Yenne
Ref. 4-11	*The UFO Phenomenon* by the Editors of Time-Life Books
Ref. 4-12	*Kryon Book 6 – Partnering with God* by Lee Carroll
Ref. 4-13	*Secrets in the Fields* by Freddy Silva
Ref. 4-14	*Star Dreams*, a film by Robert L. Nichol
Ref. 4-15	*Tuning the Diamonds* by Susan Joy Rennison

CHAPTER 5: The Energy of Creation – Its Origin

In this chapter:

Our sun at the centre of the solar system acts as a window in the veil between the hyper-dimensions and our four-dimensional space-time continuum. Through that window comes the love energy from All That Is, which humans use to create their reality. In this chapter I am going to describe how that energy travels to humans on planet Earth and how we use it in creating our reality. This information comes mostly from four communications from Angels which I channeled in 2009. The text of the four communications is given in Appendices 3, 4, 5 and 6.

The Source of the Energy

I was told by the Angels – but I think I have always known this deep in my cellular memory – that all forms of energy come from what humans call God. (We saw in Chapter 2 that the energy may or may not be condensed into matter.) As we have grown in spiritual knowledge, we have come to call that source of everything in the universe 'All That Is' – a name I first saw in the material channeled from Seth (Ref. 5-1). The more we understand about the multidimensional universe in which we find ourselves the more we realize that this universe must be made from the energy that is God. Since in the beginning there was only God, then all the galaxies and worlds that we can perceive must be derived from that one source – All That Is.

Everything I have perceived in this lifetime and everything I have been told by sources in this and other dimensions all lead to the same conclusion: God is the universe and the universe is God – All That Is.

It follows from this that any energy that comes into our part of the universe must come from All That Is. That energy is part of All That Is. For reasons we do not understand yet, the energy appears to flow down to our four-dimensional world from the higher dimensions numbered five through twelve, what Richard Hoagland (Ref. 5-2) calls the hyper-dimensions. In Appendix 3 the Angels tell me: "Those hyper-dimensions encompass us, the Angels and civilizations of beings on different planets that have learned to travel through some of those hyper-dimensions. Your Earth story that you call Star-Trek has fantasized about traveling from one part of the galaxy to another via the hyper-dimensions. This is done routinely by many civilizations around the galaxy. In due course so will the people of Earth."

Energies from Hyper-Dimensions

There are three forms of energy that come to us from hyper-dimensions:

- Love energy
- Electromagnetism
- Gravity

The division of the hyper-dimensional energy into these three forms does not occur until it reaches our four-dimensional space-time.

I will tell you what the Angels and my Guides have said about each of these energy forms. Let's start with gravity because it is the simplest:

Gravity

Although this force comes from hyper-dimensions, it is the weakest because it is stepped down so much. However, it is very necessary because without it we humans would not be able to remain on the surface of our planet; we and our planet's atmosphere and oceans would be thrown off into space by the centrifugal force produced by the spinning of Earth. That's how we can put satellites into orbit around the Earth: we send them there by a rocket that travels just fast enough for its centrifugal force to be balanced by the pull back to the Earth's surface by gravity.

Gravity is a force of attraction between pieces of matter. My Guides tell me that:

Gravity is an interaction between particles of matter.
The energy for the interaction comes through the atoms.
It gets into the atoms via the hyper-dimensions.

All the matter in the solar system and the universe consists of atoms. As we saw in Chapter 2, parts of the atoms' structure are in other dimensions and it is through those parts of the atoms that the hyper-dimensional energy is fed, causing the attraction of gravity between atoms. Of course, the amount of gravitational attraction depends on the size of the lump of matter. For the moon the gravitational force is 1.6 newtons, for the Earth 9.8 newtons and for giant Jupiter 24.9 newtons. (Ref. 5-3)

Electromagnetism

This is the second most powerful form of energy that comes to us from hyper-dimensions. I am told by the Angels that all the electromagnetic energy comes to Earth from the hyper-dimensions though our sun. We can consider this energy in two parts:

- Magnetism
- Electromagnetic energy, for example, light

I talked about both of these energy forms in Chapter 2. So here's a quick review of the main points:

Magnetism:

- Magnets don't have to be recharged. You can put a magnet on your 'fridge,' leave it undisturbed for ten years and when you return it will still be hanging on.
- If you magnetize ten pieces of iron by stroking each one with a magnet, they all gain magnetic energy which will attract other pieces of iron or steel to them. But the original magnet retains its strength.
- Electricity is made by rotating a coil of wire in a magnetic field. People thought that the electricity was coming from the rotational energy. But in the mid 1800s British scientist Michael Faraday noticed that if a metal disc, in place of the wire coil, was rotated in a magnetic field that was also rotating at the same speed – i.e., the disc was stationary relative to the magnetic field – the device still produced electricity (Ref. 5-2).
- The above observations suggested to James Clerk Maxwell – Faraday's friend – that the energy came from another dimension (Ref. 5-4). In 1921, Albert Einstein encouraged a mathematician, Theodor Kaluza, to publish this as evidence for the existence of a fifth dimension (Ref. 5-5).

Knowing the above facts, we should not be surprised when the Angels tell me, "Principally there is a force you call magnetic which comes to Earth through the sun from Sirius. As your scientists rightly guessed, magnetic energy is a form of hyper-dimensional energy."

They go on to say, "The energy that is fed into your electrical systems in different countries of your Earth comes from two sources. As you tell the children in your science workshops, one source is the sun light which creates potential energy by placing water in high places so that when it is fed into a turbine it creates the spin that is necessary to rotate your generator armature (the coil in which electricity is generated). But that is only part of the energy and we would say that is a relatively minor part. The major part of the energy that is fed into the electrical systems of your planet comes from the hyper-dimensions in the form of magnetism, which is the force that drives the electrons around the circuits creating the energy you regard as electricity." (Appendix 3)

My Guides agree with this account of electricity generation. They described it slightly differently, saying that the electrons that constitute electricity are there before and after the electricity is used. The electrons can be considered the 'working fluid' of electricity – like water is the working fluid in a steam engine. We can conclude that most of the energy of electricity comes from hyper-dimensions via the magnetic field in the generator.

Next the Angels told me about the importance of magnetism for our biology:
"That magnetic energy is available to you at all times and is not only critical for generating electricity but, as you have been told by Kryon, it is necessary to operate your living systems because your DNA and all the workings of your cells are attuned to a constant supply of magnetic energy. It is as if the DNA in your cells was constantly bathed in magnetic energy and from this is derived the energy of life or consciousness. It is a special gift to you from All That Is." (From Appendix 3)

Electromagnetic energy:

Continuing the main points in Chapter 2:

- We saw that the energy of love had a frequency of 10^{33} hertz. Now the Angels have told me (Appendix 4) that 10^{33} hertz is the changeover point. Below this frequency the energy is considered electromagnetic and above that frequency the energy is pure love.

- Putting the above another way, we can state that the hyper-dimensional energy that is stepped down in intensity until it reaches a frequency of 10^{33} hertz or lower becomes electromagnetic energy. Energy remaining at a higher frequency is still love energy.

- The electromagnetic energy that is created by the stepping down process radiates from our sun as sunlight but it consists of a lot more than just visible light.

- In the electromagnetic spectrum the band of frequencies that we see as light is very narrow. In (Ref. 5-6) it is suggested that if the full electromagnetic spectrum were a line about two meters long, then visible light would be a band about one millimeter wide. Some of the more familiar kinds of electromagnetic radiation are shown in Figure 2-4.

- Electromagnetic energy travels as waves in a magnetic field and waves in an electric field. The magnetic field and electric field are at 90 degrees to each other and to the direction of travel of the electromagnetic wave, see Figure 2-3. James Clerk Maxwell showed that the electric field and magnetic field create each other very rapidly as the electromagnetic radiation travels forward (Ref. 5-3).

Love Energy

The hyper-dimensional energy is stepped down in intensity to make it acceptable to humans by the strange loop ladder – described later in this chapter. If its frequency remains above 10^{33} hertz, then it is regarded by the Angels (Appendix 4) as pure love energy. Below that frequency the energy becomes electromagnetic.

Because the four galaxy window stars, the double star Sirius and our sun are all rotating, the love energy comes to us in the form of a spiral. The Angels often refer to this as spiral energy. In addition to the differences in intensity – referred to as frequency in the

86

electromagnetic case – the form in which the energy vibrates is the main difference. In the case of the electromagnetic energy it vibrates as a wave, with amplitude varying in a dimension perpendicular to the direction of propagation. In the case of the love energy it vibrates along a spiral; the pulses of greater or lesser intensity run around the spiral so they can be considered longitudinal pulses (Appendix 4). (For a non-scientific analogy I refer you to a later section of this chapter titled Physical Nature of Spiral Love Energy.)

Many humans are already familiar with love energy. They know it as the 'Love of God' in the context of their religious beliefs, at least in the Western world. It seems to me that this is the same thing as 'subtle energy' which is the way some scientists refer to it.

The scientific literature on these subtle forms of energy has been growing for about sixty years. The pattern that is emerging is that in the western scientific literature the love energy is referred to as 'scalar' and in Russian studies as 'torsion' (Ref. 5-4). But there are other names such as quantum fields, tachyon fields, Tesla waves or longitudinal waves – the latter name agreeing with the Angel description in the previous paragraph. It seems likely that the differences seen by scientists relate to the circumstances of their observations.

Let me briefly describe the characteristics of each kind of energy:

Scalar Fields

The scalar field has been considered to be a component of the electromagnetic field, which is always there but it is undetected because it is masked by the electromagnetic field. Experimentally, you can let two electromagnetic waves cancel each other – by arranging the crests of one wave to be superimposed on the troughs of another wave. What you are left with is a scalar field which consists of information held as vibrational energy patterns. Once again this agrees with what the Angels are telling me – love energy is the same thing as information. An analogy that may help in imagining a scalar field is a whirlpool which appears static but the water flowing through it is very dynamic. Scalar energy appears as a static pattern but inside the pattern the energy is vibrating and constantly moving. (Ref. 5-4)

The scalar information field may be the basis of Rupert Sheldrake's morphic fields, which are theorized to contain all the information needed by living systems – humans, animals, plants, crystals and molecules – to reproduce and grow the form of their species. For example, we can plant a cutting of a willow tree – a little sliver of willow wood – and under the right conditions it will grow into a beautiful tree. The information telling the cutting how to grow into a tree is encoded in a field in, or associated with, the cells of the cutting. (Ref. 5-7) It seems that the scalar fields are also the basis of the templates injected into the four dimensions of the Earth plane by Angels. This was discussed near the end of Chapter 3.

My Guides provide confirmation after the following section on torsion fields.

Torsion Fields

Like scalar fields, torsion fields transmit information at 100 times the speed of light. The main difference between them is that spin is an important characteristic of torsion fields. Since this energy has traveled to us through stars, suns and planets, which are all rotating – probably in several modes – we should not be surprised.

Since the late nineteenth century scientists have been reporting strange results that they connected with unknown fields of energy. Eventually, in 1913, Einstein and Cartan (Ref. 5-4) pulled most of these phenomena into a Torsion Field Theory but because these effects were so weak compared even to gravity – which itself is very weak – the theory was considered irrelevant to scientific research. However, that was in the days before computers and the information age. In recent years phenomena that relate to information transmission have become hot topics. You may have heard of Dr. Emoto (Ref. 5-8), a Japanese researcher who has shown that water can capture information energy coming from human consciousness. Other researchers such as Bernard Grad have shown that the 'magnetization' of water – giving it healing properties – by Mesmer in the 1700s was the same effect Emoto has discovered and both result from torsion fields generated by people (Ref. 5-4).

As Hoagland points out in (Ref. 5-9), the Russians are experts in torsion fields. They conclude that any spinning sun or planet that is moving relative to some other reference, such as the centre of the galaxy, emits dynamic torsion fields. Therefore, torsion waves propagate through the universe distributing information. This appears to be the same knowledge that the Angels are giving me!

There is evidence that all the information energy coming from hyper-dimensions has a big effect on biology – to me this is consistent with the idea that the love energy comes from God as a gift to the inhabitants of planets in the universe. We saw above that one of the manifestations of scalar fields may be the biological effect called morphic fields by Sheldrake. Russian researchers have found that torsion fields have significant effects on biology too. For example, Grebennikov is famous for his Cavernous Structures Effect (Ref. 5-4). This relates to his discovery that empty honeycombs, from wild bees, can have strong psychoenergy effects on humans with symptoms resembling the flow of Kundalini energy when it is triggered in the human body. This may be connected with the shape of structures that favor resonance or refraction of the torsion field. We will discuss biological effects of subtle energy in detail later in this chapter.

To summarize: we can see that both scalar and torsion fields – which are known in some areas as 'subtle energies' – are derived from hyper-dimensional energies. Both can have a strong influence on human biology. This is forming the basis of research into healing and a number of researchers are working in this important area. There is a large body of research into this area going on at the present time but we cannot go into the details here. I suggest that if you wish to follow up on the research on healing you look at the work of: Valerie Hunt, Barbara Ivanova and Glen Rein (Refs. 5-4; 5-10).

My Guides provide the following confirmation:

Scalar and torsion fields are the basis of Angel templates and morphic fields.
The main difference between scalar and torsion fields is the latter spin.
Understand both act in living systems.

The Path of the Energy

The energy comes into our galaxy – we call it the Milky Way – through a few stars that act as windows. I am told that there are four stars arranged at the points of a huge tetrahedron which act as hyper-dimensional windows for the galaxy. (We will see later that tetrahedrons act as transmitters and receivers for the energy.) It is through these four window stars that love energy comes into our galaxy. For planet Earth the nearest of the four window stars is the one we call Sirius or the Dog Star – appropriately the brightest star in our night sky.

Drunvalo Melchizedeck points out (Ref. 5-6) that astronomers have realized that our solar system moves through the cosmos in a spiral. So it must be gravitationally connected to some other large body. After a long search, the astronomers found that our solar system is intimately linked to the Sirius system through gravitation. (In 1862 astronomers showed that Sirius consists of two stars: Sirius A – a 'normal' star and the one we see shining brightly. Sirius B – a very dense white dwarf star, which is dark. Both stars rotate around each other. The relative rotation pattern of these two stars is part of the knowledge that the Dogon people in Mali, Africa learned from dolphin-like visitors who came from one of the planets in the Sirius system. See Chapter 4.)

To me it seems strangely appropriate to find that the star which acts as our window to the hyper-dimensions is the brightest star in our sky and that humans have past connections with some inhabitants of one of its planets. For me personally it is very appropriate because I believe my Guides have taken me on out-of-body visits to one of the Sirius planets which they call Kuzalini – but that is a topic for another book.

While we are still in the realm of galaxies and inter-galactic space, my Guides have a few things to tell us about effects which our astronomers have named supernovae and nebulae. Generally these spectacular objects, which have become much more visible to humans since the advent of the Hubble Space Telescope, are theorized to be massive currents of plasma – matter in a very high state of energy that I told you about in Chapter 4. My Guides confirm that these objects are energy currents. They say:

The energy flows you see in pictures are initiated in four dimensions by 5th dimension energy tides.

From Sirius the hyper-dimensional energy comes into our solar system via the interior of the sun and planets including Earth. Before we discuss that step in the process we need to talk about how the very powerful hyper-dimensional energy is 'stepped down' in intensity for it to be acceptable to humans. This is the function of the 'strange loop ladder.'

The Strange Loop Ladder

I first encountered this mechanism in Douglas Hofstadter's book *Godel, Escher, Bach* (Ref.5-11). The author talks about self-referencing systems in mathematics (Godel), drawing (Escher) and music (Bach). For example, M. C. Escher, the Dutch artist, has produced a drawing of an art gallery (Ref. 5-12) in which we see through a window in the drawing a picture of the same art gallery – the drawing is self-referencing.

When systems refer to themselves they move up to a higher level of power. Consider when we are learning a language – we have a basic language that refers to things and actions such as "The dog sees a rabbit." But in teaching us how to translate these words into another language the instructor has to use what is called a 'meta-language', i.e., a language transcending the common language. The instructor may say, "The verb in the sentence 'the dog sees a rabbit' is sees." That meta-language statement has more power than the original statement because it shows understanding of the mechanism of the simpler language. Hofstadter calls this self-referencing a 'strange loop.'

It seems to me that humans go through strange loops as they gain an understanding of life, and they may have to go around the loop many times before they realize they are in one and they can rise above it. For example, a person may get drunk every night and wake up 'hung over' every morning. He may be stuck in the loop of recurring behavior and be powerless to do anything about it. Then one day some event occurs that makes him realize that he is stuck in the loop and he resolves to do something about it. He has stepped outside the loop and by observing the behavior loop as something independent of himself – this is the self-reference part – he gains personal power over the loop. In effect he has graduated to a higher level of personal power.

A perfect example of a strange loop occurred when humans first left the Earth in the space programs of the 1960s. We were given a view of the Earth that no human had ever seen before and we realized how beautiful our home planet was. This was self- referencing by most of the human race and it gave us a new kind of power. I believe that's when the new energy that Kryon talks about (Ref. 5-20) started coming to the Earth.

I think it is by a series of strange loops that humanity has become aware of itself and the processes by which it learns about itself. As a result of looking back on a series of strange loops – the strange loop ladder – we have increased our personal power. Maybe this is how our consciousness has grown. Perhaps the scale of consciousness that Hawkins writes about in *Power Versus Force* (Ref. 5-13) is a measure of how far we have progressed since we humans started out as energy creatures.

In connection with self referencing the Angels have told me: **Consciousness is energy becoming aware of itself.**

Quoting now from one of the Angel communications (Appendix 3) we return to the subject of this chapter: "Because the energy that comes from Sirius is at such a high level of intensity it is necessary for that energy to be stepped down in intensity before it comes to your solar system. That is when a chain of what you call strange loops acts as a step-down transformer to bring the power down to levels acceptable to the beings on the planets in your area of the galaxy. Jacob saw a ladder leading into Heaven and Angels ascending and descending that ladder. He was seeing that same series of strange loops. ... you understand the concept of energy traveling around that loop until it becomes aware of itself. When it becomes aware of itself it moves into the next level, and so on up the ladder. The energy that comes from All That Is through the double star Sirius devolves down the ladder following the same path." This is how the energy arrives at our local sun and planets.

The sun at the centre of our planetary system acts as a window between the hyper-dimensions and our four-dimensional existence – what physicists called our 'space-time continuum'(See Chapter 2). The solar system is fed through this window by the love energy stepped down to an intensity acceptable to humans by the strange loop ladder. However, this is not the only path the energy takes to humans, some hyper-dimensional energy comes through the planets as we will see later in this chapter. My Guides tell me that the stepping down by the strange loop ladder occurs in the 5th dimension but the division into love energy, electromagnetic energy and gravitational energy – discussed earlier in this chapter – does not occur until the energy comes through the windows we call the sun and planets, i.e., into the space-time continuum.

The Path Through the Sun

The amount of energy that comes through the sun depends to a certain extent where in the galaxy the solar system is situated and in which direction, relative to Sirius, the solar system is headed. The Angels told me (Appendix 3) that the whole solar system revolves around Sirius in a long orbit. Depending on where we are in that long orbit the amount of radiation changes. The Angels say, "It is like the summer and winter of your galactic travels."

In addition to the orbit around Sirius, our planet's axis wobbles in a long circular motion, called precession, that takes about 26,000 years to complete one circuit. This is the effect that is responsible for the yugas, described in the ancient Hindu and Tibetan writings. The yugas are ages of different lengths – but of the order of one or two thousand years – during which human consciousness seems to be either asleep or awake. The direction of the Earth axis wobble, either toward or away from the centre of the galaxy, influences the amount of energy coming through the sun which has an effect on our human degree of consciousness. A great deal has been written about precession and the yugas, particularly as it relates to the energy coming to Earth at present. If you wish to read more about it I refer you to Drunvalo Melchizedek (Ref. 5-6), Richard Hoagland (Ref. 5-9).

The Role of the Planets in Bringing Energy Into the Solar System

Paraphrasing what the Angels describe in Appendix 3:

Richard Hoagland has correctly pointed out that it is not only the sun that sends energy from hyper-dimensions into the solar system. The planets receive energy from the hyper-dimensions because they too are rotating and they have at their centre a double tetrahedron that issues energy out from the planet. That is why you read that several of the planets emit more energy than they receive from the sun. For example, careful measurements show that Jupiter gives off about twice as much energy as it acquires from the sun (Ref. 5-14).

94

So it is not just a question of energy from the sun being reflected but added to that reflected energy is energy that comes from the interior of the planet. Some of that energy nourishes the planet and excess energy is sent out into the solar system and you people in the world experience this energy particularly when you consider astrology and the effects of the planets. The astrological influences that come to you on the planet Earth are the results of energy emitted by the planets. That energy that is emitted by the planets comes through their interior windows to the hyper-dimensions.

Let us talk for a while about the hyper-dimensional windows inside the planets. We have already seen references to tetrahedrons being receivers and transmitters of hyper-dimensional energy. (This will be discussed in much greater detail in a later section of this chapter.) We are told (Ref. 5-9; Appendix 4) that inside every solar system planet is a double tetrahedron, see Figure 5-1. These are not actual solid tetrahedrons but probably standing energy waves that resolve into the double tetrahedron shape. It is a fact of geometry that the points of the inscribed tetrahedrons touch the outer surface of the planet at latitudes 19.5 degrees north and south. The double tetrahedron acts as a lens for hyper-dimensional energy which issues forth from the planet's surface from at least one of the touching points.

There is visual evidence of this in the great red spot on Jupiter. This feature of Jupiter's surface has been observed for at least 300 years by Earth astronomers. Their explanation for the feature has been that there appears to be a storm – a hurricane of enormous proportions – however, they are at a loss to explain the stability of that storm for at least 300 years! Richard Hoagland (Ref. 5-9) has provided a more realistic explanation for the stability of the great red spot at 19.5 degrees south of Jupiter's equator – at least it is more realistic to the believers in hyper-dimensional energy. Jupiter is not alone in this respect, a similar spot has been observed on Neptune (Ref. 5-2).

You are probably wondering about the double tetrahedron touching points inside our planet Earth. The Hawaiian Islands are located at

19.5 degrees north of the equator. The Hawaiian Islands have been formed over many millennia by the lava issuing from a hot spot in the Earth's crust. And what causes that hot spot in the Earth's crust? Hyper-dimensional energy! In addition, it is generally recognized by many people that Hawaii is a very spiritual place, as you would imagine a land would be if it is balanced on a fountain of hyper-dimensional energy. Two other spiritual places close to 19.5 degrees north and south are Mecca in Saudi Arabia and Ayers Rock in Australia. The lack of precision in the location of these places relative to 19.5 may be due to the fact that the hyper-dimensional energy 'jet' spreads at least 5 degrees either side of 19.5 judging by Jupiter's red spot.

Feeding Energy Into the Lattice

The hyper-dimensional energy from Sirius, after being stepped down in intensity, is emitted by the sun and planets in the solar system. The Angels tell me (Appendix 5) that some of the energy emitted by the planets doubles back on itself and is 'reabsorbed' for the use of the planet for its own well being. The energy that doubles back towards the planet's surface forms a layer of hexagonal cells around the planet. Supporting evidence for such an effect comes from Richard Hoagland who reports a hexagonal 'cloud' being observed and photographed (Ref. 5-2) above Saturn's north pole by NASA's Voyager mission in the 1980s. Also, Drunvalo Melchizedek (Ref. 5-6) reports that Earth scientists have theorized a web of hexagonal cells around galaxies. This is something that comes out of the scientists' equations about the flow of energy from stars.

Of course, Earth is no exception to this. Earth sends out from the tetrahedral touching points hyper-dimensional energy which it has received internally from Sirius. That energy radiates out into space, but a portion of it curls back and feeds into a hexagonal structured lattice which is around the Earth and extends throughout the universe. In the hexagonal structure lattice or matrix is stored a great deal of energy and information that humans on Earth can access. This is what Kryon refers to as the Cosmic Lattice (Ref. 5-15).

Gregg Braden calls it the 'Divine Matrix' (Ref. 5-16). It is a web of information and energy, which are essentially the same thing – we could call it information energy. That information energy exists right throughout the universe in several dimensions at one time. So the cosmic lattice should not be thought of as being a physical thing of four-dimensional existence. We are told by Kryon that it exists in all twelve dimensions of which the universe consists, yet only part of it shows up in Earth's four dimensions. (See Chapter 7 for a detailed description of the cosmic lattice.)

Part of the information energy is contributed by the people of Earth. All the humans that have had lifetimes on Earth leave their collected wisdom, understanding and learning and deposit it in the hexagonal lattice structure. I believe this is what is referred to in different contexts as the Web of Knowing, the Collective Unconscious or the Akashic Record. It is a depository of the information that has been gathered in all the lifetimes of all the humans that have lived on the Earth. There is a great deal of information that has been gathered and stored there.

All the information energy is available to all the humans who have a lifetime on Earth at present. They can resonate with different parts of the lattice and from it they can obtain energy which they can use to create their futures. They can also obtain information from the lattice to help solve problems or create new things for the Earth. I shall be discussing the mechanism of withdrawing creative energy from the lattice in Chapter 7.

When a human partakes of that energy, borrows it or uses it, it does not lessen the sum total of the information in the lattice. You can think of the lattice as being a library where humans can go and borrow a book – the Angels suggest that is what humans do when they resonate with part of the lattice – information comes to the human but at the same time the information stored in the library is not lessened by the resonating exchange with the human. The lattice is not reduced in its power; in fact, the opposite happens. As each human resonates with the lattice and receives information from it then the outcome of the human's spiritual processes – which you would probably think of as mental processes in creating something – is fed back to the lattice and adds to its sum total of knowledge.

That is the total story of how the energy forms those hexagonal structures that have been glimpsed by scientists either in a practical or a theoretical situation. They've got their ideas about the hexagonal lattice from their own lattice. So we could say the lattice is informing people about its own existence. That is a very good example of self-reference on which the strange loop ladder is based. The knowledge that comes to us knows that it exists and it is able to present itself whenever a human needs that information. The lattice is a self-regulating, self-perpetuating device that helps the beings of any planet. The same system is repeated for all the planets in the galaxy.

(Paraphrased from Appendix 5)

Astrology

If you are interested in such things I expect you have already made a connection between the energy coming from the planets and the influence on humans that we call astrology. There are two parts to this: the energy from the sun and that from the planets.

Sun

In *The Mayan Prophecies* (Ref. 5-17) Maurice Cotterell suggested that the Earth's orbit around the sun could be divided into twelve parts with a slightly different magnetic field. Depending where in the Earth's orbit, i.e., the month conception occurred, a developing fetus would be exposed to a unique combination of magnetic fields during its nine months of development. This would influence 'somehow' the personality of the newborn child in accordance with the well-established characters expected of the different astrological signs; Aries, Taurus, etc.

In 1998 Kryon explained that 'somehow' as a connection between human DNA, the genetic code and the magnetic field between the sun and Earth at different times of the year (Ref. 5-18). The essential information that was missing up to this time was that in addition to the physical double strand molecule of DNA there were ten magnetic strands wound around it. The physical parts and the magnetic parts were analogous to the hardware and software of a biological computer. The different magnetic influences that the fetus experiences during its journey in the womb around three quarters of the Earth's orbit of the sun 'programs' the magnetic part of the DNA and results in the personality characteristics of the sun signs we humans have come to expect, e.g., (Ref. 5-19).

Planets

The planets act as windows to allow hyper-dimensional energy to pass through into the solar system. Some of the energy doubles back to form the planet's lattice but the rest spreads out into the solar system, bathing the other planets, and any beings on them, in love energy. This influence is the basis of planetary astrology.

As we saw above the influence of the sun on human personalities was mainly through the magnetic form of the hyper-dimensional energy. We will now see that the effect of the planets is also based on magnetic effects. Kryon tells us (Refs. 5-20; 5-21) that astrology is the study of the magnetic alignment of our birth imprint. The imprint means that we are born into a specific spiritual energy created by the magnetic alignments of the planets and this has a predictable effect on us. Because astrology is so intimately connected with magnetic alignments, Kryon warns astrologers (Ref. 5-15) that the magnetic shift he brought about has slightly changed the settings of the astrological charts. In addition, there is a gravitational effect – we only have to remember the influence of our moon on our emotions. So we conclude that the planets affect us through hyper-dimensional energy stepped down to magnetism and gravity.

Here is Kryon's analogy describing our birth imprint and its magnetic alignment: In (Ref. 5-21) he suggests that we consider a tree that is raised in a tropical forest. If it is moved to other parts of the world, maybe to a cold dry place, it will not feel happy and will not function well. But when it returns to the conditions it knew at its 'birth,' i.e., its early years – moist and hot – it will be happy and will flourish. That's what astrology does. It defines the conditions that existed at your birth, relative to the sun and each planet, and tells you when those influences are recreating some or all of the conditions of your birth so you can feel happy in them and prosper in all senses.

Physical Nature of Spiral Love Energy

We have seen before, in Chapter 2, that light and all electromagnetic radiation consists of waves in two dimensions. One dimension is the direction of propagation and the other is perpendicular to it. I know that Figure 2-3 shows two waves at right angles to each other, but if we separate the electric vibration from the magnetic vibration we see that they each travel as two dimensional waves.

Hyper-dimensional energy stepped down in intensity – what we call love energy – is different. Because it comes through stars, the sun and planets which are rotating the love energy wave is in the form of a spiral. (Remember Richard Hoagland's pun on the real estate maxim – "When it comes to hyper-dimensional energy, everything is rotation, rotation, rotation" [Ref. 5-9]). Love energy waves travel in three dimensions, the direction of propagation and two dimensions perpendicular to it. Think of a Slinky spring toy and you will have a good analogy for the appearance of the traveling love energy.

My Guides also tell me that above the top electromagnetic frequency – 10^{33} hertz – the energy vibrations change to pulses instead of waves. So now – if you think like a physicist – you can see it as a longitudinal wave with pulses of greater and lesser energy going past any point in the spiral. If you don't think like a physicist, imagine a hose pipe wound in a spiral around a reel and the tap to which the hose is connected is being turned on and off very fast. Then the pulses of water in the hose are like the pulses of energy coming to Earth in that spiral love energy.

At this point, for the readers who are interested in fundamental physics explanations, I refer you to Appendix 1. In that my Guides explain about biasing the zero point energy to reduce inertia in a counter-clockwise direction of the spiral. They say that humans who are creating anything spin counter-clockwise love energy into their creations. We will talk about the spiral energy of creativity in Chapter 7.

Humans and all living things on Earth interact with spiral love energy from the Creator. That is why spiral forms are so common in nature. Think about:

- Distribution of seeds in pine cones (viewed from the top of the cone).
- Sea shells like the nautilus.
- Arrangement of florets in a daisy or sunflower centre.
- Cellulose molecules that are laid down helically in wood fibers in trees.
- The DNA instructions for making a human, animal or plant in a double helix.

In 1986, some researchers at Sydney University discovered a spiral trace in a polymer film on a glass plate. It was interpreted as hard physical evidence of spiral energy being delivered to a carbon particle in the centre of the film (Ref. 5-4). When I was writing this section I was considering contacting Dr. Barsamian – the researcher who discovered it – for permission to include his photograph in my book. As I sat looking at the picture in the reference my Guides' voices came in my head, "You have one in your thesis!" I got out my Ph.D. thesis from 1961 at Manchester University and flipped through the photomicrographs of crystals forming in dye films deposited on glass plates. There I found the photomicrograph in Figure 5-2.

My Guides said through the pendulum:

This photograph shows a spiral arrangement of crystals in a film of dye molecules on a glass surface.

In the centre of the spiral crystal array is a bigger crystal attracting the spiral energy.

Thank you Dear Guides for showing me this photo that was waiting for me for nearly fifty years! I will tell you more about this 'coincidence' in Chapter 7.

Tetrahedrons as Spiral Energy Lenses

A tetrahedron is a solid geometric figure with four triangular faces. Pyramids, like Egyptian pyramids with four base sides, are double tetrahedrons – the base line common to the two tetrahedrons is the diagonal of the square pyramid base. Another format for a double tetrahedron is that shown in Figure 5-1, which is a hypothetical structure inside each planet of the solar system (Ref. 5-9). I am told by the Angels that the most important part of the tetrahedron for gathering spiral energy is the triangular faces. Whatever the size of the spiral there is always some part of the triangle – we're talking about separation of the sides of the triangle – that can resonate with some part of the energy vibrating along its spiral path. So the triangle is a universal antenna for any spiral energy.

I am told (Appendix 4) that whatever material they are made of, be it glass, stone or metal, the tetrahedrons refract the energy waves that come from the hyper-dimensions via Sirius. It's like light being refracted by a glass of water – light is bent because it travels slower in water than air, that's why a straight straw in a glass of water looks bent – in this case the spiral energy travels a little slower as it enters the material of the tetrahedron and so it is refracted into the interior of the tetrahedron. The tetrahedron acts as a lens – although strictly speaking it is not a lens – for the spiral energy that comes from the hyper-dimensions. As a result, the tetrahedrons draw into their interior some of the energy that is flowing around them.

The bigger the tetrahedron, the greater is the amount of energy that can be gathered. Really small tetrahedrons – like the small pyramidal devices that people make to collect energy and retransmit

102

it – can pick up small amounts of energy. Of course, really large tetrahedrons like the pyramids on Earth can pick up much larger amounts of energy. It does not matter whether the pyramid has smooth sides or steps, the same process works in each case. The Mayan step pyramids are just as effective at gathering hyper-dimensional energy as are the Egyptian pyramids.

In the Egyptian pyramids it is known that the focus – of the tetrahedron considered as a lens – is called the King's Chamber. But this is a misnomer because it was never intended that the king or pharaoh would have his body put there. Instead it was a place where people like the pharaoh, and other people of high standing in the Egyptian society, could go and receive energy from hyper-dimensions. As a result, they could go out of body and experience other dimensions through the energy that was beamed into them at that focus called the King's Chamber.

The Angels continue (Appendix 4);
"All those energies from the sun and all the planets come to your Earth and are available for picking up by tetrahedrons. The Egyptians, the Mayans, and the Atlanteans and Lemurians before them, knew about this energy and that is why pyramids are such an important part of their societies. They realized that these buildings or devices could act as lenses and focus the hyper-dimensional energy for the benefit of the people in those societies. That is why you are beginning to know about the pyramids on Mars, because those societies of Atlantis and Lemuria, and others before that had prior existence on the fourth planet out from the sun, which you call Mars. They already knew when they lived there that the hyper-dimensional energy could be gathered in that way. That is why those tetrahedral structures were assembled on Mars. As Richard Hoagland has correctly suggested, there is a very strong connection between the society that existed on Mars and the society that you call Egypt. The face on Mars and the Sphinx of Egypt both originate from the same society and historical concepts that were carried from Mars to Earth by Spirit. That is of historical interest and support for Richard Hoagland's theories."

Merkabas

Now I include another section of the Angels' communication (Appendix 4) that starts with a reference to the double tetrahedron structure in the planets as shown in Figure 5-1.

"We talked about the double tetrahedrons in the planets as a refresher of what we said last time. Also this is an introduction to a double tetrahedron, which is much more applicable to humans. Of course we are talking about the double tetrahedron structure of the merkaba, or energy body, which is around some humans. Those energy structures have been drawn and modeled by Drunvalo Melchizedek (Ref. 5-6) and he has explained in great detail those tetrahedral structures, which are themselves made of energy existing around the human body. Of course, you humans can't see those structures until you become attuned to focusing on that particular form of energy. The energy that is used to construct the merkaba around humans is similar in characteristics to the energy that is beaming in from the sun and planets into your Earth plane and is picked up by humans."

"As soon as humans give intent to live a spiritual life they receive a merkaba around their bodies (Refs. 5-22; 5-6). It is quite small to start with but it is constructed from energy that has come from the sun and planets in the form of a spiral. Once a person has received a merkaba, and realized that they have it, then they can absorb more energy using it because the double tetrahedral structure of the merkaba acts as a lens to bring in more spiral energy as it comes from the sun and planets. Once the energy tetrahedrons have been set up around a human it is possible for the human to gather more energy and to grow their tetrahedral structure to an enormous size. In your Earth measurements you would say that from one side to another is of the order of fifty feet in a very well-developed merkaba. Yours Malcolm is of the order of twenty-five feet. You are doing very well but you are at the beginning of this process of absorbing energy. The more you understand about this the more energy you will absorb, the greater will become your merkaba and therefore the

104

more energy that it can absorb. So it increases in an exponential way once you start that process of growing your merkaba."

Love Energy Interacts with Biology – Transmutation and Manifestation of Atoms

Having been trained as a chemist, I have often wondered how our bodies make the particular proteins – there are hundreds in our bodies – that are needed in any particular location. It always seemed unlikely to me that exactly the right proteins will be available from the raw materials that are present in the diet of the person.

For example, when cells divide the double helix pair of DNA molecules zip apart like a zip fastener. One side of the zip fastener goes with the new cell and the other side remains with the parent cell. That means that a new single strand of DNA has to be built in each cell to complete the pair. Each cell's processes must assemble a certain array of the four basic proteins – adenine, thymine, cytosine and guanine – to continue replicating its DNA. Nature – God – has realized that it is highly unlikely that the necessary atoms are present in the required numbers to form whatever compounds are required and so it becomes necessary to manifest the required atoms. That is where love energy comes in and provides that requirement. Here's what the Angels told me about how that works (Appendix 6).

(A word to those not familiar with chemistry – atoms are bonded to each other to form molecules, which are the basis of matter, including the stuff our bodies are made of. Really big molecules are called macromolecules.)

The love energy transmutes existing atoms and/or manifests atoms by transforming energy to provide the right kind of atoms at the reaction site so that the necessary molecules can be made from them. For example, if there were insufficient oxygen atoms available from molecules in the body's food but there were many hydrogen and carbon atoms available, then the love energy would make more oxygen atoms by transmuting some of the carbon atoms. Those

105

extra oxygen atoms that had just been manifested by the addition of love energy to the carbon atoms can then be used to build the necessary molecules that are required in that reaction and that particular area of the body.

The most important compounds that are facilitating these kinds of reactions are the enzymes. There are thousands of different enzymes in a human body and each has a specific chemical reaction to facilitate. Part of that facilitation is assembling the right numbers of atoms to build the compound for which the enzyme is specific. If the enzyme has not got the right number of atoms to assemble into the required molecule it brings in love energy, which manifests itself as the required atoms. Then those atoms can be built by the enzyme into the necessary molecule which in many cases is fitted into the still larger macromolecule needed in the body. For example, the protein base materials that are fitted into the DNA chain as described above.

Here comes the really miraculous part!

How do you think the love energy is gathered by the interacting enzymes and molecules? The chemical bonds of a carbon atom form a TETRAHEDRON! Figure 5-3 shows a model of a methane molecule, which consists of one carbon atom bonded to four hydrogen atoms. If you draw lines connecting the hydrogen atoms, a tetrahedron is formed.

Just as the galaxy has a tetrahedral arrangement of energy stars; the interior of planets have tetrahedral energy structures; pyramids and merkabas have tetrahedral structures so carbon atoms have tetrahedral structures. Those tetrahedral structures make it possible for love energy to be gathered by carbon atoms because they act as antennae for the love energy as it flows through the bodies of humans. That is why all life forms on Earth – animals and plants – are based on the chemistry of carbon.

As the Angels say, "This is something that has been devised by the Creator and you would probably say that it seems miraculous. It is miraculous that it all fits together so beautifully and it works without any problems whatsoever."

My Guides add:

- *Element transmutation is common to all life forms.*
- *Not only humans, but animals and plants, use love energy to manifest required atoms.*

The transmutation of elements sounds rather like an alchemist's dream. But there is evidence that this is a capability of some bacteria. Certain types of bacteria – e.g., *Deinococcus radiodurans* – can devour radioactive wastes and render them harmless. This process – called bioremediation – was predicted by Kryon (Ref. 5-20) and may be used to clean up some of the worst radioactive waste sites (Ref. 5-15).

Another explanation that comes out of this miraculous application of love energy concerns people known as 'breatharians.' These are people who claim they can live without food (Ref. 5-24). Now we can see how this may be possible. By absorbing love energy, which is transformed into atoms and molecules, we can see how they may be able to maintain their bodies without obvious nutrition.

The Angels finish this section of their communication (Appendix 6) this way:

"Once the chemistry has been started and the human body is growing well, through chemistry the synthesis of necessary molecules continues unabated and unnoticed by the human. All that's known is the human has to eat nutritious foods and those get converted into body material."

Love Energy and Healing

Not all of the love energy that is gathered by the carbon atoms' tetrahedral structures is needed to act as raw material for the synthesis of proteins and other molecules. Some of it is fed into the body and is used as energy by the body. There are two forms of energy available to the body, which come from that love energy. One of the forms the love energy can take is that called 'Chi' or 'Prana' – the name depends on the culture. Traditionally in many countries this is the energy of life. It is the energy that flows around the human body in the meridians and is used, for example, by people that do acupuncture. They channel the Chi energy in a way to cure various diseases of the body. It is quite miraculous to see the cures that result. But the mechanism of that miracle is that the Chi energy is channeled into making changes in the physical structure of the body.

Sometimes it is not necessary for an acupuncture specialist to divert those Chi flows; instead, the person can bring about the miracle themselves. You hear of miraculous cures which come about because the person – through intent, through their faith – believes that they can cure themselves. The individual human brings that love energy through the body to the point where it is needed. The enzymes, which we talked about earlier, take over and from that energy manifest the required molecular structure in the area to bring about the necessary cure.

Bodies are able to repair themselves as long as they have a human spirit in them to give intent to cure the body. You may have seen photographs of religious adepts in other cultures. For example, in some parts of Hindu culture adepts can put metal rods through the flesh of their cheeks, arms and chests. Apparently they feel no pain and when the metal rods are removed the flesh is healed immediately. This is another example of love energy manifesting the required molecules in this case at the point of removal of the metal rods.

Love energy can be received by healers and directed into the bodies of willing recipients. The healers change the molecular structure at the points in the body to which the energy is applied by the same process that we have been talking about – manifesting from love energy the required physical atoms and molecules in the right configuration to provide a cure for the human body.

I asked my Guides if they could make clearer the different ways love energy is utilized in healing. Since most of them were involved with science in at least one of their lifetimes on Earth, they appreciate diagrams. So they gave me the following, which I think summarizes quite nicely the previous section.

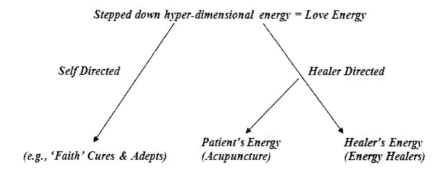

All those healing techniques depend on bringing in love energy and applying it so that the necessary molecules and structures of a healthy body are manifested from the energy. In Chapter 4 I talked about Angel energy being manipulated and condensed into matter manifesting, for example, miraculous pictures on a cloak or on a wall. When adepts materialize objects from apparently nothing, they are using the same technique of bringing that love energy in and creating a molecular structure that is perceived as the object that is manifested.

All these miraculous things are based on the same mechanism – that of love energy coming into the Earth plane and condensing into atoms, molecules and structures that are part of healthy human bodies, objects or pictures from which humans can receive a message. It is the same spiritual chemistry in all those situations. These miraculous phenomena are a great gift from All That Is.

References for Chapter 5

Ref. 5-1   *Seth Speaks* by Jane Roberts
Ref. 5-2   *The Monuments of Mars* by Richard C. Hoagland
Ref. 5-3   *Physics Today* Published by World Book, Inc.
Ref. 5-4   *Tuning the Diamonds* by Susan Joy Rennison
Ref. 5-5   *Einstein* by Walter Isaacson
Ref. 5-6   *The Ancient Secret of the Flower of Life Volumes 1 & 2* by Drunvalo Melchizedek
Ref. 5-7   *The Presence of the Past* by Rupert Sheldrake
Ref. 5-8   *The Hidden Messages in Water* by Masaru Emoto
Ref. 5-9   *The Hyperdimensional Election of Barack Obama and 2012*, DVD by Richard C. Hoagland
Ref. 5-10   *Infinite Mind* by Valerie V. Hunt
Ref. 5-11   *Godel, Escher, Bach* by Douglas R. Hofstadter
Ref. 5-12   *The Graphic Work* by M.C. Escher
Ref. 5-13   *Power Versus Force* by David Hawkins
Ref. 5-14   *The Planets* by Carl Sagan and Jonathan Norton Leonard, Published by Time-Life Books
Ref. 5-15   *Kryon Book 7 – Letters from Home* by Lee Carroll
Ref. 5-16   *The Divine Matrix* by Gregg Braden
Ref. 5-17   *The Mayan Prophecies* by Adrian G. Gilbert & Maurice M. Cotterell
Ref. 5-18   *Kryon Book 6 – Partnering with God* by Lee Carroll
Ref. 5-19   *Sun Signs* by Linda Goodman
Ref. 5-20   *Kryon Book 2 – Don't Think Like a Human* by Lee Carroll
Ref. 5-21   *Kryon Book 1 – The End Times* by Lee Carroll
Ref. 5-22   *Kryon Book 3 – Alchemy of the Human Spirit* by Lee Carroll
Ref. 5-23   *Organic Chemistry* by John McMurry
Ref. 5-24   *Breatharians* http://en.wikipedia.org/wiki/Inedia

CHAPTER 6: The Dual Human

In this chapter:

Out of Body Experiences

Many people have had experiences that seem to be explained by the concept of out-of-body traveling. When I was in my thirties, I started to experience my spirit being out of my body. I used to wake up, shortly after I had gone to sleep in bed, and find myself in some other part of the house. But the strange thing was I couldn't switch any lights on or off because my fingers went through the switches! Then I realized that I was out of my body and, with a sudden feeling of panic, I zoomed back to my body, still lying asleep, hovered over it for a split second and slipped back in with a thud that woke it up.

After a few trips like this I got used to this out-of-body routine and I decided to experiment. One evening I was unable to attend one of the psychic meetings that I talked about in Chapter 1, so I decided to visit the couple that ran them via an out-of-body trip.

Feeling something like Santa Claus, I slipped through the roof into their house. The very sensitive wife detected my presence and we had a short telepathic conversation in which I suggested she ask her husband, who worked at the same research centre as me, to mention my visit the next day. As soon as I walked into work the next morning he greeted me with news of how my 'visit' was noticed.

The record, at least in my family, for distance in out of body travel goes to my son Adam. When he was about 16 years old he traveled out of body from Vancouver, Canada to Iwakuni, Japan, where I was on a business trip, and observed his mother and me. About two weeks later, he made a similar trip from Vancouver to Melbourne, Australia where our travels had taken us. On our return home he told me the details of the activities he saw us involved in. These activities were not routine. In Japan he observed me dressed in a kimono while a woman brought soup to the hotel room for my wife who was sick. In Australia he saw us and two other people help a fifth person who had just been involved in a canoeing accident; in fact, Adam saw the canoeing accident from his view point above the trees along Melbourne's River Yarra. I was amazed by the precision with which Adam was able to describe the incidents and I told him that every detail was correct and the events he saw took place just as he had described.

This ability to travel out of body at will is not confined to a few individuals. There are accounts by ordinary people who never thought of traveling out of their bodies until they found themselves in special circumstances, for example, undergoing a surgical procedure under conventional anesthetics. The physical aspects of the surgical procedures were quite normal by modern standards but what was abnormal was that some aspect of the patient's consciousness saw and remembered seeing their body undergoing the surgery. In many cases the patients later gave an account of all that happened in the physical operating theatre including, in some cases, a verbatim account of what was said by the operating theatre staff.

The ability of humans to travel out of their body and to remember what they see has been well documented. For thousands of years shamans have been doing this to help native people hunt for food. Modern governments of some countries have set up programs to train certain suitable individuals in their military to go out of body on observation missions. A book describing the work and problems of these remote viewers, as they are called in the United States, is *Psychic Warrior* by David Morehouse (Ref. 6-1). There is even a book giving 'How To' lessons on cultivating this ability; it is *Soul Traveler* by Albert Taylor (Ref. 6-2).

The experiences of the remote viewers have shown (Ref. 6-3) that some part of human beings – we'll call it the spirit – can travel out of body to places as far away as other planets in the solar system. Not only can they travel in space but, also, back and forward in time. This makes sense with humans being projections into four-dimensional space-time from higher dimensions as my Guides describe in Chapter 2. It seems that once free of the condensed energy of our bodies, we can travel anywhere in the universe.

The Two Beings That Fuse to Make a Human

You may wonder why I am describing these out-of-body experiences in detail. The main point that I want to make is that our spirit is a sentient being that can observe, reason, plan and remember without a body. The images I saw in my house when I first left my body – like my hand going through the light switch – are as clear today as they were forty years ago. Yet those images were not perceived by physical eyes nor remembered by a physical brain! So why do we need a physical brain? It is because human existence consists of two parts; a spirit being and a physical being. The latter, what we refer to as our body, is just a vehicle – a very sophisticated, skilled vehicle but nonetheless just a vehicle. The two parts are fused together at birth and often do not separate again until death.

The Angels tell me that the true power behind the body is the human spirit. They say (Appendix 8), "You are right in thinking that the human spirit comes directly from its home in what you regard as the 5th dimension. It is free to roam over many dimensions when it is in what we shall call its ground state, it is your normal state when you are between lifetimes on any planet. ... That spirit has all the powers of a sentient being, it reasons, it remembers, it makes plans, it looks through other lifetimes and it learns through its experiences in those lifetimes."

"When you are in spirit, without a body, then all you have to do to think about something is to touch upon the relevant part of the cosmic lattice. All the memories are stored in the cosmic lattice and you resonate with the lattice – we all do that. If you need to think about some particular item, what you on Earth call strawberry jam, for example, just the mere idea of something like that leads you to the part of the cosmic lattice where the information on strawberry jam is residing and resonating. You are able to resonate with it and that becomes a thought. You have the ability to recall those thoughts – what you call on Earth memory. All those powers are available to the human spirit."

(I will describe the cosmic lattice in detail in Chapter 7: **The Energy of Creation – How We Use It**.)

"When a spirit decides to come into a physical body for a lifetime on a planet, and there are many different forms of physical bodies that can be taken, some very solid and others only partially solidified – as you know all bodies consist of energy. When a spirit decides to take on a body it selects parents who will conceive the body and the spirit is helped into the body as a human."

In Chapter 3 my Guides explained the process by which a spirit body and a physical body are combined. They said:

Usually the starting guides and the oversoul (of the new human) meet with the parents' oversouls.
This is done as the act of insemination occurs.
This leads to DNA from the father and the mother combining.

114

The combined DNA creates a portal (in the veil – see chapter 2 for description of this effect) *through which the oversoul injects a template.*
The template conveys the information to the molecules forming the body.

(I have just restated my Guide's words on the energy part of this process. There is more to this important process, such as the agreement that is formed between the starting Guides and the human's oversoul or Golden Angel. In addition, there is much more in the template than just molecular instructions. I refer you to Chapter 3 for those details.)

At this point we can see that what we have in our beings as Earth humans are two forms of energy. Our starting point was that the only thing that exists in the universe is energy – we call that energy All That Is or God. That energy exists in different forms depending on how fast it vibrates, i.e., its frequency of vibration. It seems to me that the energy that constitutes the spirit part of our being vibrates at a higher frequency than the energy that is condensed into the matter of our physical being – our bodies. In fact, for those of us that like scientific diagrams, I suggest we can represent the energy distribution of a living human being as a bimodal distribution, Figure 6-1.

The main point that I want you to understand from this discussion is that we humans are all made from the energy that is God. So we all have that Divine Spirit within us.

Walk Ins

In another related context we are told that on occasions – which may be rare – another driver can come along and take over a vehicle that is no longer needed by the original owner. We refer to this as a soul change. Ruth Montgomery discusses the evidence for this in her book *Strangers Among Us* (Ref. 6-4).

The Relationship Between the Spirit and the Vehicle

My Guides say:

The only reason a spirit needs a body is to experience physical life on a planet.

Here are some more points that my Guides made about this relationship:

When a human needs help the spirit being calls 911.
Help is on the way immediately.
Frequently humans do not believe in spiritual matters.
In such cases the physical being does not recognize the spiritual being.
In which case communication with the world of spirit is not possible.
Physically the non-believer does not pray.
Prayer can be defined as the physical being talking to the spiritual being.
Of course the spiritual being represents All That Is or God within us.
In the case where the physical being connects with the spiritual being help is always available.
The original act of the physical being connecting with the spiritual being is called finding yourself.

Angels add (Appendix 8):

"When the spirit steps into a body it is just like the driver stepping into a car. It is a very sophisticated car that tends to think it is the boss, but in actual fact it is a very elaborate computer that the spirit manipulates in order to experience physical life. Sometimes that spiritual being becomes a little lost in the drama in which it is taking part as a human body and we want you Malcolm to point out that the spirit is the true 'me' in the human body. That true 'me' is the spirit that came from the 5th dimension and all the roles the body can play are valuable lessons but they should not be confused with being the true existence."

116

Coming back to the vehicle analogy, a car could be thought of as being conscious on some level because it has a computer that can do useful things like reminding us to switch off the lights when we leave it – or even switching them off for us if we have an expensive car. But in the case of the human body, those are really just reflexes which can seem very intelligent because, for most people, the body/vehicle we 'drive' is a fine machine made by the best manufacturer in the universe. But because it is so fine we sometimes confuse it with the real us. We tend to talk about the body as 'me' and think we are all the things that the body experiences like fear and anger. We say, "I am angry," not, "My body feels angry." This is the physical being talking – what we used to call the personality or ego. It's just like our car reminding us to switch off the lights.

Really our true existence is the spiritual being, which I think has all the lofty qualities of the mind including a sense of humour. We are meant to live above the controlling function of the body; that is just the car's computer which can, and often does, think it's running the whole show. If we let it, it will take over and get us involved in all kinds of experiences, like jealousy and resentment.

An extreme example is when the body becomes addicted to some substance or sensation, then the physical being really does run the show to the detriment of the spiritual being, which often has great difficulty in reasserting its control. The spiritual being needs to remain aloof of such actions and the extent to which it can is measured, I think, by the level of consciousness as defined in *Power Versus Force* by David Hawkins (Ref. 6-5). The spiritual being needs to be frequently checking the physical being observing it like the driver of the car checks the instruments. It is one thing to check the level of gas in the tank and another to become so involved that we say, "I'm running out of gas."

The Actor Analogy

The Angels have another way of looking at the spiritual being and physical being relationship (Appendix 8). I will let them tell it in their own words:

117

"Another analogy that comes to us is actors in a play. The actor is the spirit that comes to the theatre and puts on a costume and takes a part in a play. That is what you do when you come from the 5th dimension as spirit and enter a body, you put on a costume. You are taking part in a play on the surface of the planet Earth. You learn from that experience of being in the play and interacting with the other people, the other beings on the planet. Some of the beings are Angels (although you do not always recognize them as such) but sometimes it's necessary for a critical part in the play to come forward – then an Angel will appear as a human. You, Malcolm, have experienced this quite recently with the man that came to your talk a few months ago who reminded you about zero point energy – you realized that he was an Angel. Sometimes it's necessary for an Angel to come along and give a hint to one of the actors in the play as to how the play should develop, that's what was happening in that case."

"The important thing to remember is while you are on the surface of this planet, while you are in the play, it is only a play. It is not the whole game, it is not all that there is, because after the play is over you take off those costumes – what you call die – then you go back to your spirit existence with all the memories of the time in the play. The experiences you gained in the play are still with you. So your true 'brain,' your true understanding resides in your spirit. The physical brain of the body you occupy is just a very elaborate, very wonderful, very miraculous computer that you learn to operate as a spirit driver or as a spirit actor."

"Sometimes in that play some people take on the part of a villain and they may do something very bad, such as kill someone else, but that is necessary for the play to progress and for other people to learn from that. When the actors gather after the performance and have a party and laugh about interactions, then the murderer often chats with the murdered person and they both understand what it is that they had to do with each other while they were in the play. Other than the experience that was gained the play is over now and the actors have gone back to their dressing rooms. They

118

celebrate, they think what a wonderful experience it was but they are glad they are not in the play all the time. Because that is what many people on the planet Earth at the present time are suffering from, they are trapped in the play. As Kryon says, "They think the camouflage is real!" We know that the camouflage is just part of the scenery on the stage. The actors are wearing costumes to make them look like regular humans. But if they give some thought to it they realize that they all have experience beyond the play when they go back to become spirit beings once more."

Extra-Terrestrials and Their Technology of Spirit

We are told by Kryon (Ref. 6-6) that the universe is teeming with life, so we should not be surprised to hear that many types of aliens visit Earth environs. It is apparent from some horrific abduction accounts that we should establish protection against the minority of aliens that mean us harm. From my personal experience and from what I have read, I conclude that the majority of alien abductions are spiritual and beneficial. This leads me to propose the following generalization: in most bad abductions the human body and spirit is taken, whereas in the beneficial abduction cases only the spirit is taken on board the UFO.

My Guides confirm this as follows:

Bingo you have defined the difference between good and bad intent abductions.
Some good intent abductions take the body and spirit too.
Bad intent always take both.

My reason for introducing this topic at this point is that I believe the meager evidence shows some aliens have technology for separating a human spirit from its body. If so, it shows that they, the aliens, have a greater understanding than humans of the relationship between the body and spirit. The book *The Watchers* by Raymond Fowler (Ref. 6-7) tells us that on several occasions Betty Andreasson's spirit was taken out of her body by an alien wielding one of two types of handheld devices. In early abductions, the device was a small ball of light that an alien projected to her forehead. In a later abduction, the device was a small box that the alien placed on the couch where Betty was lying, reading her bible. In this case, Betty remembered standing there in spirit and looking at her body, which continued to sit and read the bible she had been reading when the aliens came into her mobile home through the wall. Betty saw that her body turned the pages of the bible as she left in spirit form – through the wall – for a trip with the aliens in their craft. When she returned, her body lay there with the bible on its stomach, apparently asleep.

In this book (Ref. 6-7) there is a whole chapter on out-of-body experiences connected with alien visits leading to abductions, which almost in every occasion seemed to be of the beneficial kind. In one remarkable instance Betty and her husband, Bob Luca, were simultaneously taken out of their bodies by vibrations emitted by an overhead UFO. They saw each other leave their bodies, which were left standing in the bedroom while their spirit forms clung to each other as they passed through the ceiling on their way to join the UFO. They were returned safely to their bodies later by the aliens.

The aliens also told Betty that their technology was concerned with spirit. It seems they have learned to manipulate the energies that constitute the consciousness that we refer to as spirit. What the Angels call, "Energy that has become aware of itself."

My UFO Experiences

Betty states that her abduction experiences started as a child. I had UFO-connected experiences as a child, from about the age of nine, which I always interpreted as dreams. However, as I grew older, particularly after my out-of-body experiences that I described earlier, I became more convinced that they were also out-of-body experiences. Typically the experience followed the same pattern:

I knew I could climb out of my bedroom window onto the sloping roof over the kitchen. I could walk down this roof until I reached

120

the fence that divided our garden from our next door neighbours' garden. From there I could easily climb to the ground. (I had practiced this route as a fire escape – if you think this is a strange responsibility for a nine-year-old child to take on, please remember I had survived World War II bombing raids by this time.) However, in every dream I <u>floated</u> down the roof and over the wall into the parking yard of a six-story apartment block – which we called 'flats' – at the bottom of our garden. In the parking yard was the alien craft, which I never saw as being any particular shape, but I remember it had many coloured lights around it. I floated into the craft where I met tall beings that seemed like adult humans to me. The craft would take off gently at first and I and a group of children, already on board, would watch on a big screen the ground falling away beneath us.

The whole group of children was shown many things – I seem to remember being shown lands that appeared foreign, some very dry dusty places with sharp angular rocks – they could well have been on alien planets. I seem to remember the travel rather than the lessons. The whole atmosphere on the ship was one of calm efficiency, very much like I imagine the bridge of a cruise ship to be. There seemed to be about twenty crew members – male and female – and they all appeared to be kind, normal humans. Nothing frightening was ever done that I remember. In the morning I would wake up in my bedroom – sometimes shivering, lying on the floor under the window.

Two memories that came to me after each of these dreams: one was a sensation of 'vibration,' like finger nails scraping down a blackboard, and the second was the feeling of effortless power as the craft took off. As an adult, I rode in helicopters many times and as they took off I always recalled that feeling from my dreams.

When I started to experience out-of-body travel, as I have already described, then I started to question whether these were really 'just dreams' because these experiences had a common quality. This was particularly noticeable in the floating mode of travel and

121

the passing through solid walls and roofs. I even recognized the 'blackboard/fingernail vibration' as being associated with my spirit leaving my body. Imagine my surprise when a few years ago I met a lady – at a psychics class – that I recognized. She had the same feeling about me and we quickly placed each other as one of the children on the alien craft. That lady was Marjorie, who found her pendulum wrapped in her newspaper delivered to her front door (Chapter 3).

Recently the Angels confirmed (Appendix 8) these dreams were educational flights as follows:

"One of the ways that you came out of the body was when you were trained by what you would call aliens or interplanetary beings – who are also inter-dimensional beings – and who travel between dimensions and help young humans learn about the existence which we all share. You remember being on the craft and the dreams you had about the experiences on the craft and in fact those were not dreams as such – although you remember them as that – but in fact they were out-of-body experiences. Your childhood colleague, Marjorie, traveled in those same craft with you. You remember each other from being in the craft together with several other children being shown wonders of the universe. You understood so much of what was happening around you in the world from a spiritual point of view. You, Marjorie and the other children learned your spiritual lessons while you were in physical body on Earth."

Spirit Prompts the Physical

I expect you have had that experience of trying to recall a name. I have found the frequency of that experience increases with age. The frustrating thing is we know somewhere in our being what the word is, we know for example it is short and even the letter it starts with. We say, "It's on the tip of my tongue." What I think is happening is that the spirit can easily imagine the word and can 'prompt' the physical, which just needs to relax its efforts to do it alone. We have just reviewed an analogy of the spirit being an actor

122

and putting on a physical costume for a play on Earth. That analogy can be extended to include the spirit acting as prompter for its own physical character.

The prompting that the spirit provides takes the form of conceptual hints because the spirit deals not in building block words but in complete ideas. Here's an example: I was driving to a lake near my home to go for a run. I knew the turnoff from the highway I was following but, not having been there lately, I couldn't remember the actual street name. As I drove, I saw in my mind's eye a misty island with knights riding down paths to the beach. I turned into the road leading to the lake and saw it was called Avalon Street.

A much more dramatic example of this effect was experienced by Dr. Jill Bolte, a brain anatomist, who experienced a massive stroke on the left side of her brain. The stroke effectively cut off her access to words and symbols – the language of the left side of the human brain. She found herself in a pure spiritual existence that was serene, where she felt a great expansive peace but she knew in some part of her being that something was wrong and she needed help. She describes in (Ref. 6-8) how she had to use her spiritual intelligence to match the symbols, i.e., numbers, on a business card with the symbols on her phone to call for help.

Dr. Bolte was admitted to hospital and her mother was called – I think this is a beautiful part of her story – when her mother arrived she had the wonderful understanding that she could only communicate with her daughter's spirit. The mother got into bed with her daughter and held her in her arms. No words between them were possible or required.

You will be glad to hear that Dr. Bolte recovered completely after several years of rehabilitation. Her spirit reprogrammed her vehicle's computer so that she was able to function again as a complete and brilliant human. Now she can tell the world of her experience of interacting with the physical world entirely as spirit essence with a minimum of physical camouflage to get in the way.

Where the Spirit Resides

I already knew from such experiences as *Drawing on the Right Side of the Brain* (Ref. 6-9) that the creative, dreamy abilities of humans are usually focused in the right side of the brain. The left side usually takes care of language, calculating and controlling many of the body's conscious functions. However, I didn't know how or where the spirit connected with the brain so I asked my Guides.

Here's what they said:

90 percent of the right side of the brain is in another dimension.
The spirit operates the physical through that part of the brain.
The left side is all in four-dimensional space-time.
At birth the body is controlled by the left side.
Higher functions grow as spirit makes its presence felt.
This usually occurs at puberty.
At age twelve you were told to run and never smoke.
That was your spirit setting rules for this lifetime.
The spirit is concentrated in the right side of the brain.
But it is also in every cell.
It is like an electron cloud in a molecule.
Its probability of existence is higher on the right side of the brain.
As you see this is a description of the human quantum field.

The Human Quantum Field

In that last segment my Guides gave a perfect segue into the next topic. Those readers who have seen the film *What The Bleep Do We Know* (Ref. 6-10) will probably remember Dr. Joe Dispenza talking about how each morning he creates his day. At one point he says, "I'm infecting the quantum field" – what do you think he meant by his 'quantum field'? Here's what the Angels told me in Appendix 9.

"We have to start with the light that is issued from all the cells of your body. Yes, even the blood cells as they move around your body are giving off light as well. As your scientist Popp (Ref. 6-11) (See

124

Chapter 2) found all human cells – and all living cells too for that matter, in plants as well as animals – give off light. In the human body that light travels between the cells as a form of communication. It is a very precise, exquisite form of communication because it depends on the tiny openings in the cell walls called tubules – at least that's what humans call them. That light travels from the cell interior where it is generated by cellular reactions through the tubules so that all the cells join in one body-wide communication. This communication consists of one great standing wave of light. (See Chapter 2 for a description of analogous standing sound waves in a bowed violin string.) The light from the cells resonates throughout the structure of the human body creating a standing wave of light."

"The frequency of that vibration depends on the state of mind of the human – as we will see you can change that frequency by the way you think about your world and your existence. If you are in a happy state of mind then that frequency is high. You speak of your vibrations being raised. If you are in a poor state of mind as a result of sadness or bad news, or even worse depression, then your vibration frequency is low. That is what is meant by 'feeling low' it means that the vibration rate of the light standing wave in your body is at a low frequency. You can change your rate of vibration by one of several strategies. The one that we always recommend to people when they are starting out in this area is by being thankful; by showing gratitude for your present situation. Nothing works so well to raise the vibration rate of the light in your body like being grateful for your existence."

You will see later in this book that it is important to keep the vibration rate of the light standing wave in your quantum field high because all humans send out light probes – like insect feelers – to connect with the cosmic lattice for energy to create their physical existence. The frequency of the energy that is returned from the lattice matches the energy of the light feelers. So if you send out happy energy feelers you will receive happy energy which will manifest as good events in your life. Conversely if you send out sad energy feelers you will get back sad energy that manifests as more bad luck. This effect is called the Law of Attraction (Refs. 6-12, 6-13). You will find this process discussed in greater detail in Chapter 7 'The Energy of Creation – How We Use It.'

The Quantum Field – Home of the Spirit

While the primary purpose for this light quantum field is for communication between the cells of the body, it is much more than that. It is every human's contact with the cosmic lattice – as we have just seen – but even more important the quantum field is the home of your spirit while you are on Earth.

I will let the Angels continue from Appendix 9:
"Your spirit is energy, as you know. That energy of the human spirit combines with the energy that is vibrating in the form of light and the two together become the complete human quantum field. As you know the spirit has consciousness. It is energy that is aware of itself and that is what we call consciousness. The spirit is aware and revels in the joy it finds at being able to exist in the form of a human and experience life in a physical situation on a planet called Earth. But there are many other planets where spirits live in similar vehicles for the enjoyment and the learning that they can achieve in those physical worlds. Spirit moves through this quantum light field and attends to the heavenly needs of the body."

"The physical needs of the body are taken care of by the physical being that comes into existence at birth. The human spirit does not need to attend to the body because, as you have described before, it is like an automatic computer controlled machine. It is very subtle and sophisticated and is able to care for itself and do many of the things that spirit needs it to do with great precision. We have talked about this before in that if you wish your body to throw a ball or shoot an arrow the detailed calculations of how to hold the body in order to maximize the effect of those actions is best left to the body. It has – as you would call it in your technology terms – an automatic guidance system. It is quite capable of directing a projectile to a particular target with great accuracy. You recognize

126

that as the mechanism that is generally referred to as Zen."

"Those are requirements of the body which are subsidiary to our present discussion. This information we are giving you is about how the spirit interacts with the human quantum field. We must say before we go much further that the spirit does not have to stay within the quantum field. As many of you have experienced the spirit is quite able to leave the quantum field of the body and travel to other parts of the planet, to other planets or even to other times within your four-dimensional space-time. The spirit has the flexibility and the freedom to travel and then it can return to the body that it occupies if that is what is required. But sometimes when a spirit leaves its body it does not return and that is the event you call death. But most of the time when you go on an out-of-body experience – an OBE as you call it – you expect to return and you do so."

"Some people have seen a silver cord that connects the living body to the spirit. When the spirit is away from the body that silver cord stretches out through the cosmic lattice and keeps the body and spirit connected. That is the same effect that your physicists call quantum entanglement (Einstein's 'spooky action at a distance' -MKS) because they see a similar kind of connection between sub-atomic particles that have interacted in some way. But we will not digress into atomic physics at present. We just note these things in passing."

"As the physical body gets older and the spirit becomes more experienced it travels more out of the body. Then you reach a point where it seems that there is no spirit present in the body much of the time. This is the stage that people get to with advanced age – as they approach 100 years of age, maybe some much earlier than that – in which their spirit is not present in the body most of the time. Then the body has difficulty recalling from its physical memories many things because the spirit is not there to prompt it. This is the stage that humans go through called dementia which is a precursor to death usually – not always but in many cases. Not all humans go through that stage, some retain the full connection between their spirit and their physical memories right up to the incidence of their death of old age. There are many different possibilities depending on the requirements of the particular human and the experience that it intends to gain while in schoolhouse Earth."

The Quantum Internet – Interaction of the Spirit and Brain

The Angels explain (Appendix 9):
"Now we want to talk about, when the body is functioning well, how the spirit operates the body through the quantum field. In that book *The Field* (Ref. 6-3) – which is quite correct in most of its details – you were given the analogy of the Internet which you understand is an overall result of many computers joining together. You could say that the effect of all the cells in your body joining together through this light field has the same effect as an internet which is created in your body. The light interacting between the trillions of cells in your body is just like the electronic communication between all the computers on the Internet."

"The spirit knows where all the web sites of interest are. That's because the spirit creates many of those web sites of interest by forming parcels of energy in the quantum field which vibrate with a certain frequency. These are connected with the cosmic lattice of course. There is complete connectivity between each human quantum field and the cosmic lattice. The spirit in any particular body forms nodes of energy and in that energy is stored the information about an event or object and that is what you call a memory. Just as you have memory sites in your computer so the human spirit forms – what we will call – web sites for each individual memory that is stored in the overall human memory."

"The human brain has a physical representation of that internet stored in it. This is the physical part of the memory system. Let us say that each memory that is stored in the quantum field has a physical counterpart in the human brain. That is the part of the memory, which includes instructions and past training, which the body uses when it performs routine tasks. A good example

128

that you touched on once was learning a musical instrument. The human spirit decides that it would like to express emotions in the form of sound waves which you call music. It puts the thought into a quantum internet web site that the body should acquire an instrument and practice it. The body, especially one that is happy and joyful, readily agrees to do this. Physically it acquires an instrument and starts to practice. The spirit helps the body with the practice and receives energy from the music that is created and that energy is passed through the body. That is why you always feel warm when you play your instruments. That is the physical effect of the energy that comes through the music. As the body becomes more proficient at playing the instrument more and more memories are created; the memories of each of the tunes that the body learned. First of all the spirit records those memories in the quantum internet and a reflection of those memories are stored in the physical human brain. This means that the body has the capacity to play the instrument automatically. The body has at its disposal in the brain's memory cells a knowledge of all the tunes that have been practiced and the body can, quite automatically like a machine, reproduce those tunes on the instrument. But that is rather a bland, soul-less piece of music to other humans and it is not until the spirit's quantum memory unites with the brain's physical memory that the true spiritual emotion of the music is expressed in physical sound. The very best of the spirit and the body combines in situations like this to produce those memories both spiritual and mental and when those are aligned it is a very powerful source of beauty that stirs emotions in other humans as they receive that message of love. That's what music is, a message of love."

"We have explained how the brain is set up with memories by the spirit. When the body is first given birth it has no memories. It is not until the spirit comes into the body – which usually is at the time of birth but may be delayed as you know – that it starts to create those memory nodes in the quantum field. It starts to build its quantum internet which constitutes spiritual memory which is reflected by physical memory. The child starts to learn how to walk and speak and builds its physical memory on which it can rely for

Figure 1-1. Pictographs from Barrier Canyon, Utah

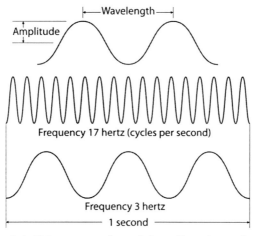

Figure 2.1. Waves produced by vibration of energy

Vibration facts:
- Amplitude is the height of a wave above midpoint
- Longer wavelengths occur at lower frequencies
- Higher frequencies mean shorter wavelengths
- Higher frequencies radiate more energy (more pulses per second)

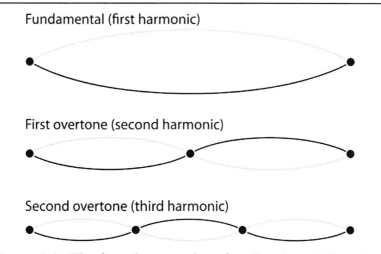

Figure 2-2. The first three modes of a vibrating violin string

Black dots represent nodes or points of zero displacement. Each mode produces a different frequency. These and other modes combine to give us the characteristic rich sounds of violins.

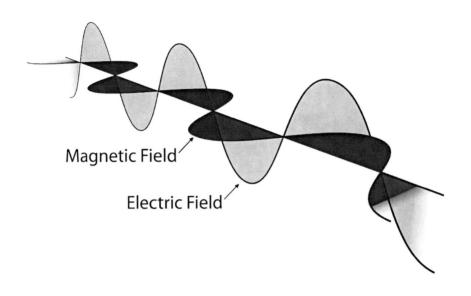

Magnetic Field

Electric Field

Figure 2-3. Light traveling as an electromagnetic wave

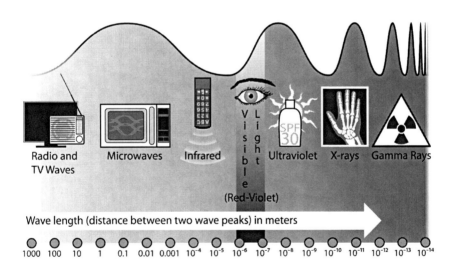

Figure 2-4. Electromagnetic wave spectrum

The Three Aspects of my Oversoul

Figure 3-1. My inter-dimensional organization chart

Figure 3-2. A kite cart – an analogy for the Angel-Guide-human relationship

Figure 4-1. Orbs at an Italian meeting

Figure 4-2. Orbs often appear on joyful occasions

Figure 4-3. My grandfather's image on his barn door

Figure 4-4. A message from the Angels?

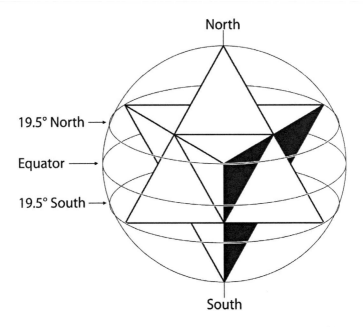

Figure 5-1. Diagram of a double tetrahedron inscribed in a sphere

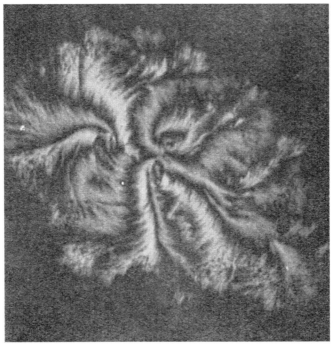

Figure 5-2. Spiral arrays of crystals in a film of dye molecules on a glass surface

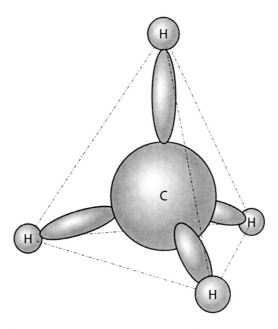

Figure 5-3. Molecular model of methane

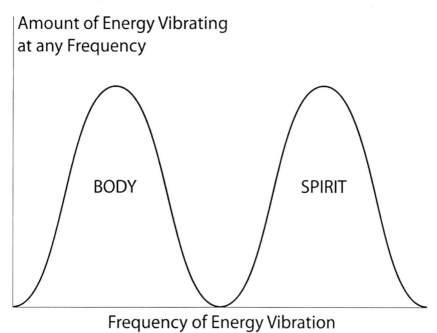

Figure 6-1. Probable energy distribution of a living human

Figure 7-1. The human electromagnetic field by Peggy Dubro

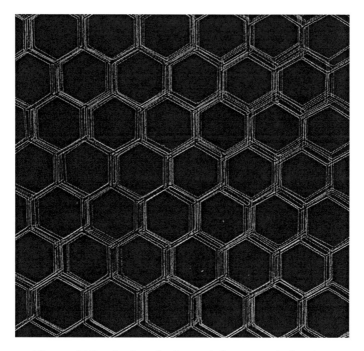

Figure 7-2. A simulation of the cosmic lattice

Figure 8-1. Silbury Hill

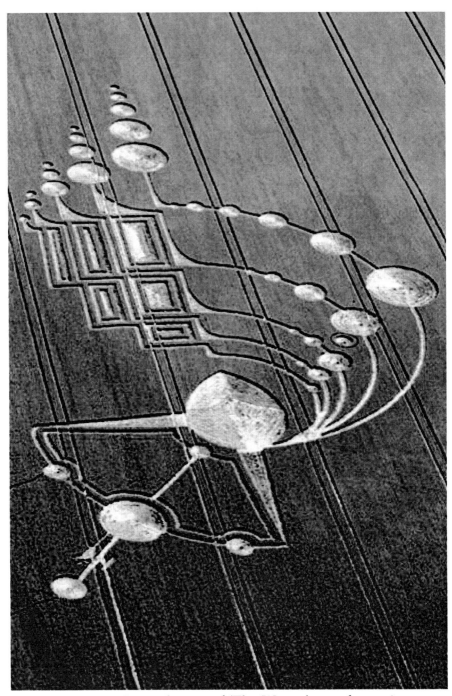

Figure 8-2. Second stage of 'The Weave' crop formation

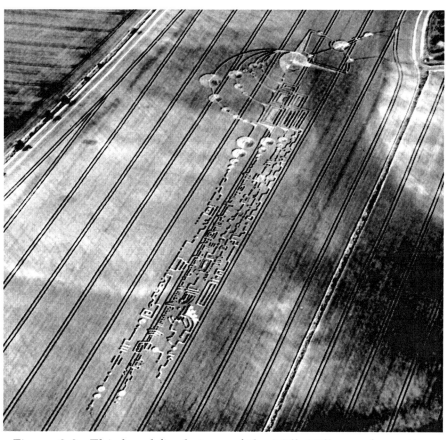

Figure 8-3. Third and final stage of the Milk Hill crop formation
(Also known as 'The Weave')

automatic processing. When the human is undertaking creative work, such as writing a book, then it relies to a certain extent on physical memory, for example how to spell words. But for its concepts – its higher thoughts – it depends on spiritual memory. To access the spiritual memory the spirit moves about in the quantum field touching on those memory nodes that it has created – in a way it is like a human clicking on web sites on the Internet. The spirit can move very quickly – much faster than the speed of light, faster than humans can comprehend – over the quantum field internet and touches on those nodes of memory that it has created. The human brain understands those memories as it receives them and translates them into words that are eventually put down on paper so that other people can read them."

"You were quite right in your recent writing that when the body needs to recall something – like the name of the street where you had to turn to the lake – then the spirit activates the quantum internet memory to provide some clues to assist the physical memory. But those clues the spirit provides are different to those that the physical brain uses to recall things. Whereas the physical brain recalls in terms of names, words and numbers the spirit recalls in terms of concepts. That is why the concept that was given in the example was of a misty island with knights riding down paths to the beach. That was the memory cue that was given from the quantum internet memory and that provided a clue to the physical body but it wasn't until the body saw the name of the street – Avalon – that it made the connection. Of course this was a demonstration of that process in action and your body received that information with great joy and recognized the value of the demonstration for understanding the mechanism."

"We are in an unusual situation, it seems that the body is writing the book but really spirit is writing about itself and how it interacts with the body. For the book we are describing the processes that we are actually using to describe the processes. This is a strange loop structure again and as a result of the self-reference this explanation gains great power." (For an explanation of strange loops see Chapter 5: **Creation Energy – Its Origin**.)

142

"Besides being a strange concept for humans to consider, this is a relatively simple process. Like all things in the universe nothing is very complex. Your physicists would make it complex because they replace spiritual understanding by mathematics. They do that because they know how to manipulate the mathematics but they do not know how to manipulate the spirit. Besides which many of them do not acknowledge existence of the spirit. The concepts – that come from their spirits – are expressed in mathematical form and in this form the body can manipulate those concepts. The difficulty with that is the body does not understand the results of the mathematical manipulation. Although the body – of the physicist – obtains equations which describe certain aspects of the universe, a true spiritual understanding of those concepts is not arrived at by that process."

Shape of the Quantum Field Occupied by Spirit

Although my Guides already told us about this earlier in this chapter the Angels provide more detail in Appendix 9 as follows:

"The shape of the quantum field is more or less fitted to the body. However, it extends outside the body to a certain extent particularly on the right side of the brain with most humans. This is because the spirit interacts most closely with the right side of the brain and traditionally that is where you get your mystical experiences, your artistic, creative thoughts. The spirit spends more time on the right side and less time on the left side of the brain because the latter is where physical thoughts, control mechanisms and physical processing of the requirements of the human body take place. All the physical activities are dealt with in the left side of the brain."

"So as your Guides explained you can imagine the energy of the vibrating light quantum field – when it is occupied by the spirit – right throughout the body but there is a preponderance of energy over the right side of the brain. In most cases psychics do not see this as part of auras because much of the extra energy is expressed in other dimensions. Spirit connects with other dimensions through this part of the quantum field. The best way to regard this is as an electron cloud in a molecule. As you know, being a chemist, the electron cloud forms into orbitals (The bonds between atoms in a molecule consist of electron orbitals – see Chapter 5, Figure 5-3 -MKS). There is a greater probability that an electron will be found in one of the orbitals than in the rest of the molecule. The orbitals can be visualized as protuberances sticking out from parts of the molecule. The human quantum field is very similar in this respect in that it has a protuberance, or an orbital, over the right side of the brain. This means that there is a greater probability that the spirit will be found in the region of the right side of the brain than in any other part of the body. But of course the spirit occupies all cells of the body, and is present everywhere in the body. It is all a question of probability of where you would be most likely to find the spirit if you were able to look."

The Two Layer Structure of Humans – Summary

"You can regard the complete human body as a two-layer structure. The first layer consists of the molecules that constitute the cells that make up the physical tissue – that is the matter part of the body. Diffused completely through that is the second layer – an energy field that consists primarily of light, and that light is what we call the human quantum field. The human spirit comes into that quantum field and lives in it most of the time. It forms nodes of memory which are in effect an energy structure paralleled by the Internet structure that you have on Earth. The spirit can touch on any of the quantum nodes – corresponding to web sites – and activate memories which are translated into physical form in the human brain. So basically it is a two-layer system; one physical and one spiritual and the two work beautifully together."

References for Chapter 6

Ref. 6-1   *Psychic Warrior* by David Morehouse
Ref. 6-2   *Soul Traveler* by Albert Taylor
Ref. 6-3   *The Field* by Lynne McTaggart
Ref. 6-4   *Strangers Among Us* by Ruth Montgomery
Ref. 6-5   *Power Versus Force* by David Hawkins
Ref. 6-6   *Kryon Book 6 – Partnering with God* by Lee Carroll
Ref. 6-7   *The Watchers* by Raymond E. Fowler
Ref. 6-8   *My Stroke of Insight* by Jill Bolte Taylor
            Also www.mystrokeofinsight.com
Ref. 6-9   *Drawing on the Right Side of the Brain* by Betty
            Edward
Ref. 6-10   *What the Bleep Do We Know?* www.whatthebleep.com
Ref. 6-11   S.Cohen and F.A.Popp: "Biophoton emission of the
            human body."
            Journal of Photochemistry and Photobiology B 40
            (1997), 187-189.
            www.lifescientists.de/publication/pub2003-04-1.htm
Ref. 6-12   *The Law of Attraction* by Michael Losier
Ref. 6-13   *The Law of Attraction* by Esther & Jerry Hicks

CHAPTER 7: The Energy of Creation – How We Use It

In this chapter:

I have found that events are often put on our life's path to act as signposts. You may be familiar with the feeling that some event, person or place has special meaning for you. I'll give you an example: In 1964 I was working as a chemist in the Research Centre of a paper company in Melbourne, Australia. One afternoon I was in the centre's library reading technical journals relevant to my research when I read a news item about a merger between MacMillan Bloedel and Powell River companies in Canada. I had never heard of either of these companies but, at the time, the item almost jumped off the page for me as it aroused that familiar feeling of being a special signpost for my life's path. Ten years later I came to Canada and started work as a chemist with MacMillan Bloedel Research.

I think it is beneficial to learn to recognize these spiritual signposts because this is one of the ways our Spirit Guides get in touch with us to help us follow our life's path. But in my case my Guides didn't just put signposts in my path, they surrounded them with coincidences. Coincidences are widely recognized as important in spiritual work. James Redfield's *Celestine Prophecy* (Ref. 7-1) suggests that when coincidences occur, you should be on the lookout for spiritual path signposts.

Coincidences

Coincidences are made of apparently normal events that would not surprise us if we experienced them in isolation. What surprises us, or quite often shocks us, is when two events with similar meanings or implications occur at the same time. There are some famous coincidences (Refs.7-2, 7-3). One I like involves the psychiatrist Jung; the fact that a scientist of his reputation talked about it seems to have legitimized coincidence as a topic worthy of study.

Jung was in his consulting room listening to a young female patient who was describing a dream about being given a golden scarab beetle as a brooch. He was sitting with his back to the window when he suddenly heard a tapping on the window. He went to the window to see what was making the noise. Imagine his surprise when he found a golden scarab beetle was repeatedly flying against the glass. Apparently the young woman took this as a sign and immediately started on the road to recovery.

When people hear about such events they usually say, "Oh, that's just coincidence!" That's the way they sweep such events under the mental carpet. But if you look deeper you will see that all they have done is give an unexplained event a name. It's like Isaac Newton, hit on the head by a falling apple, saying, "Oh, that's just gravity!"

When Guides or beings in other dimensions want to get our attention, this is one of the ways they use. In my experience, coincidence is a flag alerting me to an upcoming communication, demonstration

148

or confirmation of some new aspect of my life. I think that our Guides, being in other dimensions, are able to manipulate the timing of events in our four dimensions. They can bring apparently innocuous events into juxtaposition in such a way that the result gives us a jolt. If we are mentally prepared we can say, "I am about to receive information relevant to my needs."

Elegance and Jokes

Often, coincidences bring together two, or more, things that we have not seen together before. In scientific circles, when two or more facts are explained by a simple idea that's called 'elegance.' A common human reaction to elegance is laughter – have you noticed that people often laugh at a coincidence? That's why we laugh at jokes (Ref. 7-4). A joke is an example of elegance in the juxtapositioning of two or more different elements that the person who 'gets' the joke never thought of putting together before.

Here's an example: The scene is the 1948 Olympic Games in London, England. Those Olympics were held before strict security was necessary for such events. Three guys – an Englishman, a Scotsman and an Irishman – all without any money, were watching the competitors' entrance to the games. They noticed that all each competitor had to do was give his name, country and sporting event to the gatekeeper and they were let in without any problems. Since they all wanted to see something of the games the three cast about on a nearby building site for some ideas on how they could trick their way into the games. The Englishman found a 5-foot length of rebar – steel bar for reinforcing concrete – wrapped it in paper, marched up to the gate and announced, "Smith, England, javelin!" The gatekeeper let him in. The Scot found a round lighting fixture which he wrapped in paper and then told the gatekeeper, "McTavish, Scotland, discus!" and he was admitted. The Irishman thought that this was too easy. He cast about and found a roll of wire netting. With the netting under his arm he marched up to the gate and said, "Murphy, Ireland, fencing!"

I hope that gave you a laugh. If it did, you were holding the two very different meanings of the word *fencing* in your mind as you 'got' the joke. That's an example of elegance, which we are about to see is an important element in creative acts. Jokes and coincidences work in much the same way and in my experience so do creative acts. When we are creative we often bring a problem and its solution together.

Creative Enterprises

I've been involved in creative problem solving in my technical career and I've noticed that when you finally 'see' the answer coming out in your thought processes there's a moment when you hold the problem and the answer in your mind simultaneously. Then you see the elegance and the usual reaction is laughter. We exclaim, "Of course! Why didn't I think of that earlier?"

I've been in group creativity sessions – Synectics sessions (Ref. 7-5) that I wrote about in connection with the Library Angel in Chapter 3. On one occasion, I was in a group of five participants and we all knew that the solution to the problem was coming, although at that point, nobody could say what the solution was. We just knew it was close and we had to be patient and 'play' it like an angler plays a fish before he can get it into his net. That session was being videotaped from another room by instructors in the Synectics technique and later they asked us what was happening at one point when we five started to become excited and laughed a lot. We responded, "You had to be in the room! We all knew the answer was coming, it was just that nobody had drawn it on the board yet." It was a very psychic or spiritual experience. I think we had experienced the 'wave of intent' that I described in Chapter 2.

There's not much difference between creativity in arts and science. Einstein treated the exploratory phase of his research as an art, for example, he imagined riding on a light wave. Picasso on the other hand treated his paintings as a series of experiments and kept notes on the results like a scientist (Ref. 7-6). You may have undertaken some creative enterprise such as painting, writing a poem or composing music. On the technical side, there are equally creative activities like inventing something or making a scientific discovery. Although they are not often recognized as creative, I assure you they are. I have invented a few things – for example, the micro-vacuum crystal collector that I described in Chapter 1 – and as I did I was very aware of that process I mentioned above of bringing the need and the solution together – like two parts of a coincidence.

The Creation Takes On a Life of Its Own

I, and many others, have noticed that the thing we were creating took on a life of its own. It's as if you go into your mind looking for something and suddenly there's an idea given back to you from somewhere you can't define. The idea suddenly takes on a life of its own. Andrew Wyeth, the famous American painter, had this to say about his painting *Christina's World*, "When I applied the white, it just blew me away." The thing created is not just a passive layer of paint on a surface; it becomes a living thing and tells us what it needs to become complete. It takes on a life of its own!

In the book *Synectics* (Ref.7-5) – which the Library Angel presented to me – the author William J.J. Gordon tells of a scientist tape recording his thoughts as he invents a new aircraft altimeter. He says to himself, "Funny ... now I have the feeling that this thing is on its own ... the whole idea is no longer anything to do with being mine. ... It's amazing, and this thing is no longer I ... it's as though it was taken away from me. ... This must be what people mean when they say you start writing a play and the people you put in the play just go on by themselves."

We find that artists and scientists have similar experiences as they create something. It seems that their work takes on a life of its own. My Guides tell me that this experience is the result of information coming from other dimensions. It seems this is a part of the information energy that comes from the hyper-dimensions as described in Chapter 5.

Many artists, musicians and scientists have brought new things to Earth through the creative abilities of their spirit guided by beings in other (hyper) dimensions. It seems that the spirit we call Mozart came to earth to bring us a great gift of music and, about 200 years later, the Beatles did a similar thing. I have been told that the computer was used on other planes of existence, specifically the akashic, before it was brought to the earth by people like Alan Turing (Ref. 7-7) as the machine we know so well today. In all these cases, the creative person went into inner space and searched the energies of other dimensions to find the solution that resonated with their needs.

How do we get to that inner space where so many ideas, inventions and works of art have come from? My Guides answer that question this way:

The best ideas come by resonating your personal quantum field with the cosmic lattice.

That statement is loaded with meaning. It refers to two concepts we have already met in this book.

Personal Quantum Field

I discussed this in Chapter 6. We saw that in our bodies all cells give off light – remember Popp's discoveries? (Ref 7-8) The cellular light is coherent like that from lasers and the combined effect of all our body cells resonating – communicating – with each other is to form a coherent field of energy. That is the personal quantum field that my Guides are talking about.

Figure 7-1 shows the electromagnetic field around the human body as channeled from Angels by Peggy Dubro – an associate of the Kryon Group (Ref. 7-9). She was shown that the electromagnetic field has a constant pattern consisting mostly of fibers of energy radiating from the chakras. The energy fibers form loops which act like antennae transferring energy from the cosmic lattice by resonating with its structure.

The Cosmic Lattice

In Chapter 5 we learned that the cosmic lattice is built and maintained by hyper-dimensional love energy that comes to us through Sirius, our sun and planets. We saw how the energy comes out of the planet surfaces at the touching points of the inscribed double tetrahedrons. Some of it doubles back above the planet surface forming hexagonal cells in an energy matrix.

NASA has photographed a hexagonal 'cloud' above Saturn's north pole (Ref. 7-10). I am told by my Guides:

We confirm that the hexagonal cloud seen above Saturn is part of that planet's cosmic lattice segment.
We point out that this hexagonal cell is only part of the infinite cosmic lattice.
The cosmic lattice is around and through every known body of matter in the universe.

As my Guides have stated, the cosmic lattice is everywhere in the universe: it passes through all matter. I would like to add to their definitions the following points about it that I have learned from the Kryon writings (Ref. 7-9):

- Throughout the universe is an invisible energy matrix called the cosmic lattice.
- Its twelve-sided honeycomb cells are closed like human body cells. The cells lie side by side but do not touch each other.
- The cosmic lattice is the energy source of the universe; it is the energy of Spirit; it is the energy of Love.
- It responds to human consciousness; it is the basis of telepathy. Humans and animals intuit what is happening far away by tuning in to waves on the lattice.
- Communications are virtually instantaneous; in comparison light is slow.
- The cosmic lattice is the basis of synchronicity; we use its energy to create our futures; it is the very essence of inspiration.

153

The last statement – it is the very essence of inspiration – is the key to our subjective view of the lattice and how we use it to create things. Figure 7-2 shows a representation I have made with the help of my Guides which may help you imagine the cosmic lattice. (There is a colour version on the cover of this book.) I must point out that Figure 7-2 is only a simulation model. The actual cosmic lattice is usually invisible and exists simultaneously in all twelve dimensions of the universe.

My Guides tell me that all the information we need to create anything (a painting, music, poetry, inventions, our futures) is stored on the lattice. So are the morphic fields for all the animals and plants and crystals and molecules in the world as described by Rupert Sheldrake (Ref. 7-24). For example, a cutting of a willow tree has within its atoms the cosmic lattice. Through that it has a connection to the morphic field of all willow trees, which is part of the lattice. It is this morphic field that tells the willow cutting how to grow into a beautiful tree.

In fact all morphic fields, templates or designs that exist as energy are part of the lattice. They are woven together in a way that we on Earth would call a hologram.

A hologram is a three-dimensional image, made of light, that is stored on photographic film. The image is reconstructed by shining laser light through the photographic film. Information about any part of the image is stored ALL OVER the photographic film. In fact, if you cut off the corner of the film, there's still enough information left there to recreate the whole image, all that is lost is a little definition of the image. You can even create an image from a small fraction of the original film although the picture isn't very clear. The energy fields that are part of the cosmic lattice are spread over the cosmic lattice hologram throughout the universe so they are accessible from any part of it.

Tuning In to the Lattice

I am told the information is stored in the lattice as energy vibrating at different frequencies. For example, the information on painting

154

inspiration can be thought of as energy vibrating at one frequency represented by the purple part of the lattice model, the information on music inspiration can be thought of as energy vibrating at another frequency represented by the green part of the model, etc. We can access any particular information by frequency tuning – this is like tuning a radio to an FM (frequency modulation) station. A way of looking at it is that the purple part of the lattice represents the radio waves from one FM station and the green part represents the radio waves from another FM station. Those radio waves are full of information and we can find that information by tuning our radio, which we do by turning a dial, which changes the frequency to which our radio antenna is resonating.

Following the foregoing analogy we can see that people who are creative, e.g., artists, musicians, poets and inventors, know how to tune some part of their earthly existence to the specific frequency of the lattice where information on their specialty is stored. My Guides tell me that creative people get the help of their higher self – which Kryon refers to as their Golden Angel – in accessing the part of the lattice they require for their created work. This is why they experience the feeling of going inside their bodies to get the information.

And when they are tuned in to – resonating with – the information they need they sense that feedback from the lattice, which feels like the creation, takes on a life of its own. We then say they are INSPIRED – they have literally 'breathed in' something new.

You may be wondering how creative people go about getting the help of their higher self to tune in to the lattice. I've talked to several artists, musicians and inventors about this and most of them recognize the following steps:

- PREPARATION – spending time, maybe years, really getting to know the effect required. In the case of invention or problem solving this often involves considering what other people have done and stating the present problem very clearly.

- GIVING INTENT – to create an effect or solve a problem. This is where imagination comes in. With the 'rules' of reality suspended they consider all kinds of crazy schemes. They may say something like, "Wouldn't it be fun if we could ...?"
- GOING INSIDE their bodies into 'inner space,' really a form of light meditation. Getting to this state is often assisted by listening to music – often the creative person has a favourite piece that has worked for them on previous occasions.
- ALLOWING – watchful waiting, listening. A peaceful feeling like fishing and just watching for the float to start bobbing. And when an idea starts to show itself, they know it's best not to pounce on it because that may make the idea run away. Instead, they let the idea come to them in a gentle way – like 'playing' a fish until it's in the net. This is the stage in which the request and the emerging answer are held in mind simultaneously and the thing created takes on a life of its own.

In this type of creative situation I ask Mikael, my Golden Angel, and my Guides for help in coming up with new ideas. Sometimes – at their invitation – I write out in my journal what it is that I need and they may provide help right away either through my pendulum or by putting a thought in my head. Sometimes there's a delay and the requested idea doesn't come until I'm doing something that occupies my conscious mind – like running or taking a shower.

Our DNA is Involved in the Tuning Mechanism

In Chapter 5 we saw that our human DNA is much more than just two molecular strands in a double helix. In fact, Kryon tells us (Ref. 7-11) that there are ten magnetic strands in addition to the physical strands. Since magnetism has its origin in higher dimensions, this means that the magnetic strands can pick up information from hyper-dimensions where our Guides and Angels reside. Our physical strands are fine conductors of electricity and the information is relayed from the magnetic strands to the physical by electromagnetic induction. Through this route the information comes to our bodies and brains and becomes conscious thoughts. (This process was discussed in more detail in Chapter 2 – see Communication with Other Dimensions.)

Earlier in this chapter we saw the human quantum field consisted of standing waves of light. The Angels gave Peggy Dubro diagrams of how standing waves appear as light fibers in loops extending from our chakras (Figure 7-1). My Guides say that our DNA and the electromagnetic fiber loops work together in connecting with the lattice. In fact, the loops represent the collective effort of all the DNA in all the billions of cells in our bodies. The loops act like antennae resonating with the relevant part of the lattice – don't forget the lattice is around and through our bodies – the loops transfer energy from the lattice into our bodies.

There is an important point in respect of the frequency to which the loops are tuned. We will see later in this chapter that when we are creating our future from lattice energy we have to be careful to select the right frequency that the loops are tuned to. How we do this will be covered shortly.

Before we move to that stage I want to pass on from Appendix 7 the Angels' words on this gathering of ideas from the lattice:

"When a human wants to derive energy or information from the lattice, then that person goes into an inter-dimensional connection with the lattice; goes into an inner space, you might call it, in order to resonate with the lattice. This is why it appears that inspiration comes to you from within your bodies because it is within your bodies that you form that resonating structure of your quantum field. You have the experience, the words that you say in your Western World, of going into inner space in order to resonate with the lattice and gain inspiration."

"It appears to you humans that you are given ideas. You are not sure where those ideas come from, but many of you understand that it is a spiritual experience to receive that information. You give thanks for the information, for the ideas, for the inspiration. That thanks, that understanding of the nature of the gift facilitates further connections. We would say that the more gratitude you show for the information you receive and the energy you receive, the more you can receive that energy and inspiration. Your process of resonating with the lattice becomes exercised, becomes more proficient and you are able to seek just the right kind of inspiration that you need for your tasks. It is like exercising a muscle to make it stronger. In this case the 'muscle' we are referring to is your ability to resonate your quantum field with certain parts of the lattice in order to acquire energy from it or to acquire information from it. Those two things really are the same thing it is just that for humans it is more convenient to think of them as being two separate concepts." (Appendix 7)

Creating Our Reality – The Law of Attraction

In the last section, the Angels talk about energy and information being the same thing, although we think of them as separate concepts. So far in talking about resonating with the lattice we have been talking about a more-or-less conscious process that requests help from our Golden Angel to obtain information that people require to create something new on the Earth plane.

Now we focus on an unconscious – for most people – interaction with the lattice that we all engage in practically all the time. Unlike the creative process, where we enlist the help of our higher self, we do this alone and unaided. We resonate with the lattice to gather energy to create our future reality.

An example that many of us can relate to was described in Chapter 3 – creating a parking space on a busy street – when we are in a hurry to get to an appointment we ask the Parking Angel for help and a space opens up. I suggested that what we are really doing is imagining an immediate future for ourselves that sees us successfully parked, getting out of the car, maybe putting money in a meter and being in time for our appointment.

What I am told is that we do this all the time; we create our futures from hour to hour and day to day. And we use energy from the lattice to do it. Exactly the same process works for all of us, only many people don't know it is happening. I think it is essential that we realize that the frequency of the energy vibrating in our personal quantum field that we send out – Peggy Dubro's light fiber loops – to explore the lattice determines the frequency of the energy that is returned to us from the lattice and the quality of the future that can be manifested from it.

If we are in a victimized mode, typified by low personal vibrations – of the energy in our quantum field – the light fiber antennae will be tuned to a low frequency. The lattice energy they attract will be at a low frequency and will manifest as more bad events in our lives. How many people have you heard say, "I've already had two accidents this year, there's bound to be a third." That's like a recipe for the third one to manifest. On the other hand, if we can raise our vibrations – by showing gratitude or giving intent for a positive future – our exploring antennae will resonate with higher frequency lattice energy from which will manifest the good things for which we have just given intent.

I have just described the workings of The Law of Attraction. It states: *We attract into our lives whatever we give our attention or feelings to, whether wanted or unwanted.* (Ref. 7-12 & 7-13)

Our higher selves and our Guides are waiting to help us create our futures. Moreover they give us signs that they want to do that. That's what coincidences are for.

Lattice Energy in Created Works

People resonate with the lattice and gather information/energy from it, which they apply to creative works such as visual art or music. As a result the work of art contains within it the energy derived from the lattice.

My Guides say:

It also applies to music.
It is that stored energy you feel when you hear the music.

We humans – at least some of us in the western world – are able to detect that energy because it stirs our emotions, maybe to the point of tears. We saw in Chapter 4, in connection with crop formations, how sacred geometry and music bypass our intellect and appeal straight to the emotions. We can now understand this immediacy is the result of our quantum field resonating with the lattice energy manifested in that work of art.

Certainly in my own personal experience I know the emotional effect of listening to music I love. I can become so swept up by the music that my driving concentration suffers to the same extent as it would in taking a cell phone call. Which reminds me of an item in a British newspaper I read years ago: the police had pulled over a car that appeared to be operated by a drunk driver. When the police interviewed the driver they found he was quite sober but had been "temporarily overcome by the magnificence of Rachmaninov's second piano concerto."

Most people are less affected by visual art but, under the right circumstances, some can be emotionally stirred up. Maybe you have seen the video, available on the Internet in 2009 (Ref. 7-14), called 'Vincent van Gogh,' which shows a montage of that artist's paintings accompanied by the song 'Vincent (Starry, Starry Night)'. For me that combination of energy of beautiful paintings, music and poetry has a very powerful emotional effect.

Another thing I notice about van Gogh's art is his swirling brushstrokes – particularly in 'The Starry Night' – it seems to me that Vincent was aware of the spiraling energy that came from the lattice and sometimes his brush followed it. (Ref. 7-15)

Some artists are greatly affected by the energy of their own works and those of other artists. It's as if they are changed by their contact with the lattice – they become sensitized to the energy of art. In a similar way great conductors of orchestral music are sensitized to the energy of the music they lead. Don Campbell in *The Mozart Effect* (Ref. 7-16) talks about the long working lives of many great conductors into their nineties. It seems that their health benefits from the energy of the great music in which they are immersed.

Although I do not have personal experience of it, I am told by those with acting experience that many great actors rely on energy from sources they can't define. They use this energy in 'shape shifting' themselves into a character other than their own – in fact, some of the greatest are not sure what their own character really is. I think most of us have experienced at some time a great acting performance that stirred us to tears. We wonder how a play or film can intrude in our normal life and make us experience such strong emotions of compassion or hatred. That is the result of an actor using the creative energy to such effect.

The Insertion of Lattice Energy Into Works of Art

To bring some discipline into my storytelling about energy, my Guides have given me some 'guide lines.' In Appendix 1 I have summarized for quantum physics enthusiasts their details of the mechanism of energy projection. We need not go into those details; all we need to know is that when Golden Angels, Guides and humans project energy it is in the form of a spiral and the counter-clockwise direction is favored – by the sender. They also told me that is why my pendulum rotates clockwise for yes – that is the direction in which the energy is received. (Sent counter-clockwise means received clockwise – check it with a Slinky spring toy!)

Sometimes brief glimpses of energy leaving my body come when I have been meditating, with my eyes closed, on sending energy to someone. On the back of my eyelids I see energy spirals – looking like a top view of a rotating water sprinkler – and they always rotate counter clockwise.

My Guides also said:

Every artist has energy placed in their work by their Golden Angel.

161

This means that artists are in touch with their Golden Angel – the same as higher self. That is why artists go within themselves, they do so to contact their higher selves who help the artist get the required energy/information from the lattice and impress it into their art work. This reminds me of Amanda Dunbar, who started painting wonderful pictures when she was thirteen years old. In her book *Guided by Angels* (Ref. 7-17) she says, "My Angels tell me what to paint."

The Flow of Hyper-Dimensional Energy in Creativity – The Angels Explain Fractals

When I started writing this section I felt intuitively that there was a connection with fractal geometry, so I stuck a 'Post-It' note on my computer cupboard bearing the question, "What has all this got to do with fractals?" A few days later, my Guides told me to get ready for another Angel communication, my question was about to be answered in full. I was finishing my lunch as I prepared to channel the Angels' words and I switched on the TV while I did so. A children's cartoon came on and, as I watched, I realized the story was about an Asian boy who drew pictures that came to life. Somehow the story seemed relevant to my original question. I switched off the TV and started to channel; the Angels said:

"Hello Malcolm, yes we are here ready to talk to you again. Thank you for your request for more information about the fractals and the power of the images that come from them and the energy in the images. We are going to tell you today about a single process which you saw by coincidence (haha!) in that cartoon on television today. That cartoon was showing the story from China about a little boy – Shouping in the original story – who had the ability to draw pictures and then those pictures would come to life and create reality. That is the basic idea of what we are talking about today that people can create pictures by drawing, painting and taking photographs. There is energy put into those pictures that can, under certain circumstances, come into reality with a four-dimensional effect."

"That is what happens when artists paint pictures. You are already familiar with the idea that when they do that spiral energy is put

162

into the painting. Now we are telling you that this is just a special case of a very general effect that is possible in all known creation."

"This gift comes to us from God. God created the universe by imagining it. If you like He drew a picture of the universe. By feeding the infinite energy that is God into the picture He was able to create the physical form of the universe which is much more than humans are able to comprehend. But you feel easier talking about physical things on the scale of your galaxy and solar system so that is where we will confine our talk today."

"The artists that are taking information energy from the lattice and with the help of their Golden Angel putting it in to the work of art, whatever that may be, those artists are merely following in the footsteps of All That Is. Humans and Angels are divine creatures and have the same access to energy from All That Is. Angels create templates to bear witness to this fact. Humans are becoming aware that when they create something they put into that creation the energy of All That Is so they too are bearing witness, they see it as witness to beauty and order and consciousness. When you write a book, such as yours Malcolm, you put energy into every page and that is a very good way to bear witness to the love that comes from All That Is."

"That is the basic process that you touched upon and you wished to enquire about. Now we tell you more about the structure of that energy and how it manifests itself in different dimensions, what you call fractional dimensions or fractals. When someone creates a fractal picture – like Cheryl Harnish, an artist working in Vancouver – the energy of the fractal painting manifests as a spiral and that spiral can be detected by pendulum or other dowsing means." (Appendix 7)

Examples of Spiral Energy

I once attended a meeting in Vancouver at which Cheryl Harnish (Ref. 7- 18) showed examples of her fractal art. To create this art she meditates and contacts beings in other dimensions who give her numbers, which she feeds into the equations required by the computer program that develops the pictures. She told us at the meeting that there were energy spirals in her pictures and she had arranged for a dowser to detect the energy and its effect on the auras of people looking at the projected fractal pictures. (This is an important point that we will return to later in this chapter. The energy is not only apparent in the original picture but also in projections and copies of the picture.) On her web site (Ref. 7-18) Cheryl Harnish quotes a University of Oregon study that showed certain fractals can alleviate stress by their physiological effects.

In his book *Science and the Akashic Field* (Ref. 7-19) Ervin Laszlo describes some experiments done by the British Society of Dowsers. This research showed that dowsers can pick up information that is not produced by natural means, such as the presence of water, but is projected by the mind of another person. Lines and shapes can be created by the conscious intention of one person. The lines and shapes can be detected by another person who has not been told what has been created. The dowsing equipment moves just as if the shapes were caused naturally. The shapes could be detected with accuracy of a few inches even when they were created thousands of miles away. Time also proved irrelevant because the fields remained present and stable long times – in one case three years – after their creation.

At another meeting in Vancouver that I attended, representatives of the Damanhur federation of ashrams in Italy (Ref. 7-20) described, among other things, their use of spiral energy for healing. They had developed 'machines' that were festooned with spiral coils of wire which they scanned over the body of a person requiring healing. Other people who wished healing at the Damanhur ashrams painted pictures which were reported to contain spiral forces.

Finally, we must not forget Drunvalo Melchizidek, who has lectured extensively on the importance of spiral energy in ancient cultures (Ref. 7-21). In a more recent book (Ref. 7-22) Drunvalo reports on a coil device that could clear smog from large areas of Phoenix where the inventor of the device lived.

Continuing the Angels' Explanation

Continuing now the Angels' communication, they commented on some of the above facts and experiences as follows:

"You have seen in that book by Laszlo that some dowsers don't necessarily have to create a picture but they can construct in their minds through imagination a template – maybe it's just a triangle or a three dimensional shape. We are telling you now that the construction is in the 5th dimension and that energy construct can be detected by other dowsers with their pendulums or their rods."

"All these examples we are touching on this afternoon are offshoots of the same basic concept; that conscious beings can produce energy constructs – which you refer to as templates – and those templates are at the basis of works of art. The energy constructs of the works of art by humans mainly exist in the 5th dimension but they project their power into your four dimensions that you inhabit and that is the picture that you see. Earlier your Guides told you about energy tides in the 5th dimension creating beautiful patterns in your space-time that you call nebulae – that is the same process. The dowser or the artist or Angels construct in the 5th dimension an energy template and that is projected into your space-time continuum and manifests itself as some physical thing, maybe a painting, maybe a piece of music. Maybe even a human, because we have told you already that humans are projections of templates that Angels have created. The Golden Angel creates the template and projects the energy into the four dimensions of Earth and it manifests as a human being."

Coming back to the involvement of fractals we now have an explanation of what they are and how they relate to spiral energy:

"It's all a question of projection and the analogy that we use here is that you can project on a screen a three-dimensional image – the third dimension being the depth of the picture, which is constructed by artistic means such as perspective but in actual fact it is only two dimensions that you see on the screen. As you go mentally into the picture on the screen the two dimensions become three dimensions as you become part of the picture yourself. At some point you are half immersed in the picture and half still looking at it as two dimensions and that is where the concept of fractional dimensions comes from. In that case your scientists would say you are at a fractal dimension of 2.5."

"The mathematics of fractal dimensions are quite obscure to most humans, although they see them as beautiful patterns. In fact they are usually generated by computers from a simple equation that gradually winds you along a spiral that goes from the four dimensions in which you live to the 5th dimension. That is what is happening in pictures, you are presented with spiral energy that you put into the painting. As you travel along that spiral you move along an axis that brings you from two dimensions to three dimensions to four dimensions and eventually to the 5th dimension."

"The energy spiral exists in the 5th dimension down to your four dimensions that you call space-time. The energy spiral is a way that you can access the 5th dimension – it passes through the veil. The veil is getting thinner all the time due to the planet's energy changes, soon it won't be there at all and we will have a much closer connection with you. Until that happens in a few years the energy spirals that you create in your pictures, your paintings and your music are like access tubes. By traveling down the spirals you can go into the 5th dimension and information can come from the 5th dimension into your four dimensions where it manifests itself as something such as a painting. But the concept of the painting, the basis of it, is in the energy that creates the spiral."

"You can travel in and out of that 5th dimension by moving along the spiral. As you move along the spiral so it gives rise through the mathematics to forms that are recursive – that is from one layer of forms to the next we have the same shape of form but they are at a different size. (Recursive refers to a mathematics expression each term of which is determined by applying a formula to preceding terms. -MKS) It's like looking at an aerial view of a piece of coastline, we see bays and promontories and then as you come

166

closer to the coastline you see that it is made up of smaller bays and promontories and we can go right down to a scale where individual rocks and pebbles form those apparent bays and promontories. As you know this is the basis of the fractal dimensions and at any point in the spiral, down those different sizes, as you approach the 5th dimension you can produce forms. For example in your four dimensions you can produce natural forms such as plant material and clouds. Those are two examples of manifestation of the fractal energy somewhere along that spiral." (Appendix 7)

In his video *The Colours of Infinity* (Ref. 7-23) Arthur C. Clarke, the science fact and fiction writer, compares fractal shapes with shapes that occur in nature – like ferns and seahorses. He says that fractals have great similarity with natural shapes but infinite variety – which makes them even more like nature. In the same video, Michael Barnesley, a researcher in applications of fractal geometry, gets right down to the core of the miracle of fractals. He says, "Fractal geometry can describe a cloud as simply as an architect can describe a house." He goes on to say, "This is how God created a system which gave us free will. This is the most brilliant maneuver in the universe to create something in which everything is free. How did He do that?"

The Angels have an answer:

"Where you see your tree forms you see some aspect of the template that All That Is has created for your Earth plane. All That Is conceived the idea of a planet called Earth and imagined those plants and animals that you have on your planet. He imagined them to exist at a certain level of dimensionality, at some point along the spiral energy that we are calling a template. These levels of appearance of plants and animals appear as fields of the energy that is traveling outward in a spiral form of a template. If at some point you stop the movement out along the spiral and you consider the energy that you have there it is in the form of fields. Those fields are the morphic fields that Rupert Sheldrake talks about (Ref. 7-24) (see also Chapter 5). That is the natural existence of all the things that are manifested on the surface of the Earth which come from All That Is imagining those plants and creatures on the Earth."

"You humans imitate that process because you are divine. You are part of God and have the divine spark within you. You are able to imagine similar templates. From your place in the four dimensions you project the energy spirals that create the templates up into the 5th dimension. So that the template energy is there at various levels and can manifest itself in any particular level in a pattern."

"We hope that has given you some idea of how this process works. It is a difficult thing for humans to imagine this but if you imagine the spiral as a stretched out Slinky spring you could put pictures along the spring maybe of a cloud. As you move down that spiral towards the 5th dimension you may see more basic forms of that cloud. As you approached the source of that energy you see the point at which All That Is has put the energy into the spiral flow, the concept or the original idea that was started by All That Is. As you get nearer that those cloud shapes become more basic, become less elaborate, more abstracted until they become one point when it reaches the 5th dimension. We hope that is a concept that you could model by having a Slinky spring extended with different pictures at points along the spring, each of those pictures would become simpler as you got near the end of the spring which is the origin, the idea of All That Is." (Appendix 7)

A Theory of Abstraction

During my university years, while driving at night, I noticed that I saw multiple images of white posts on a tight bend in the road. This made me realize that human sight must have a scanning mechanism embedded in it somewhere between the eyes and brain. Also around that time in my life I was very interested in art, particularly abstract painting, and I attended painting lessons. Putting these two things together I imagined – looking back I see my Guides gave me a foreshadowing – that paintings contained multiple layers of increasing abstraction as you went further into the painting. I dreamed that by taking a representational painting and scanning it – spirally – and by mathematically treating the scan information I would be able to derive an abstract version of the painting.

When I received the Angels' communication (Appendix 7) they referred back to that 'dream' as follows:

"Your idea Malcolm about the level of abstraction is that you can take a picture and travel along its energy spiral and at various points along the spiral if you look at the fractal forms that are expressed there you will see something which is abstracted from the original representation of physical form in the painting. The further you travel along the spiral the manifestations of the energy become more and more abstract. That is what your theory says and you are quite right in expressing it. We want you to work on it but at a later date. For now we would like you to express your idea in your book because it will explain about those energy spirals that people detect in paintings and pictures. Later you can work with Michelle measuring those energies and showing how they change as you move along the energy spiral to give greater and greater levels of abstraction. You move until you reach eventually in the 5th dimension a concept that is like the focus of the spiral and is where the artist's Golden Angel started the spiral when he helped a human bring the energy from the lattice."

It seems I have yet another book to write!

Spiral Energy in Photographs

We have been talking about the spiral energy put into paintings by the artist with the help of a Golden Angel. I think the natural assumption is that energy of this kind can only be placed in pictures if artistic effort is involved. But I find that is not so, in fact photographs can carry energy too. It may be that this is a different kind of energy to that which we sense around works of art, but then many photos are works of art. I don't think we know enough about this field to be able to make any general statements about the kind of energy. That is something which needs some research. All we can do at present is tell a few anecdotes that point us in the right direction.

In some photographs there appears to be personal energy of people portrayed in them. One of the more common uses of this energy is that sensed by psychics, for example, in helping police with information about missing persons. In such cases it may be that the photo has been in the possession of the person portrayed and so their energy has been absorbed by it and can be detected by a person skilled in picking up emanations from personal possessions – the technique of psychometry. However, there are cases reported of people divining names and other information of people portrayed in photos that had been in the possession of someone other than the person portrayed. For example, a grandmother shows photos of her grandchildren to a psychic who then tells details of the children that can be verified by the grandmother.

For me the most intriguing example of energy in a photo involved cats which are well known as psychic sensitives. My son Julian has two cats who insist on being close to him. Whenever possible, they sit on his lap, 'kneading' his arms with their sheathed claws. At times he lets them sleep with him except during the summer when the weather is very hot. Then they can't get at him because he keeps his bed covered by a mosquito net, because he likes the window open while he sleeps. During such a time he heard them purring under his bed, both cuddled up on something. He rescued the something which he discovered was a thirty-year old photograph of himself as a child. He realized the cats were using it as a substitute for him. It was full of small scratches where they had 'kneaded' the photo the same way as they did with his arm.

I thought that only an original photograph would have energy in it but my Guides told me that all prints made from the original photo have the same energy in them. We saw this earlier in this chapter when Cheryl Harnish projected a copy of her fractal art on a screen and the projected image had an effect on the audience. My Guides also likened this encoded energy in the photographic prints to that in music. Every performance of a beautiful piece of music affects us because we feel the energy stored in that work of art.

Finally, in this section I come back to Figure 5-2, which came from my Ph.D. thesis written in 1961. First I want to emphasize the point I made in the last paragraph; the original photo was made on a quarter size glass plate and the print in my thesis had to be a copy, but the energy was in it. When I showed my research supervisor, Dr. Egerton, the photo he suggested it would not add any scientific value to my thesis and so I should not include it. But I had a special feeling about that particular photo; I felt it was beautiful and I decided it must be included. Little did I know that nearly fifty years later it would be called into play in another kind of research.

I asked my Guides if they knew back then I would need it for the present book. Their reply was:

As we know what you plan to do in your life we can make preparations.
Very high energy was put into that picture.
In every print is a copy of the original energy.
Your Golden Angel put the energy into the negative.
Mikael knew you would need it.

References for Chapter 7

Ref. 7-1   *The Celestine Prophecy* by James Redfield
Ref. 7-2   *Coincidences* by Ken Anderson
Ref. 7-3   *The Roots of Coincidence* by Arthur Koestler
Ref. 7-4   *The Act of Creation* by Arthur Koestler
Ref. 7-5   *Synectics* by William Gordon
Ref. 7-6   *Einstein, Picasso* by Arthur I. Miller
Ref. 7-7   *Encyclopaedia Britannica*, 2001
Ref. 7-8   'Nonlocal effects of biophoton emission from the human body' by Cohen, Popp & Yan. www.lifescientists.de/publication/pub2003-04-1.htm
Ref. 7-9   *Kryon Book 7 – Letters from Home* by Lee Carroll
Ref. 7-10   *The Monuments of Mars* by Richard C. Hoagland
Ref. 7-11   *Kryon Book 6 – Partnering with God* by Lee Carroll
Ref. 7-12   *The Law of Attraction* by Michael Losier
Ref. 7-13   *The Law of Attraction* by Esther & Jerry Hicks
Ref. 7-14   Van Gogh(1)pps
Ref. 7-15   *Vincent van Gogh by Vincent van Gogh* by Victoria Charles
Ref. 7-16   *The Mozart Effect* by Don Campbell
Ref. 7-17   *Guided by Angels Divinely Inspired Paintings* by Amanda Dunbar
Ref. 7-18   www.fractalart.ca
Ref. 7-19   *Science and the Akashic Field* by Ervin Laszlo
Ref. 7-20   http://en.wikipedia.org/wiki/Federation_of_Damanhur
Ref. 7-21   *The Ancient Mystery of the Flower of Life* by Drunvalo Melchizedek
Ref. 7-22   *Living in the Heart* by Drunvalo Melchizedek
Ref. 7-23   Video: *The Colours of Infinity* by Arthur C. Clarke
Ref. 7-24   *The Presence of the Past* by Rupert Sheldrake

CHAPTER 8: The Crop Formation Message

In this chapter:

- *Where Are All the Crop Formations?*
- *Treasure Hunt*
- *My Crop Formation Experience*
- *Back in Vancouver*
- *Atlantean Connection*
- *The Message of the Crop Formation*
- *Guides' Translation of Atlantean Message in Milk Hill Crop Formation*

For many years I have had an ambition to meditate in a crop circle. In fact as soon as I saw the first photos of the modern wave of circles – and more complex formations later – I felt that here was evidence of sentient life in other dimensions. In 1991 I bought and studied *Circular Evidence* by Andrews and Delgado (Ref. 8-1) followed by several other books as they became available. The physical evidence, particularly microscopic changes in the cell structure of plants from the circles, convinced me that these were more than human artifacts. In 1995 Kryon (Ref. 8-2) told us that these were messages from Spirit that gave good information about the workings of the universe. This made great sense to me and was in line with the information I was receiving from my Guides. I knew I would one day immerse myself in the energy of those messages from other dimensions.

Where Are All the Crop Formations?

I am from the south of England, where most of the crop formations in the UK appear – although there have been many in other countries around the world – but in spite of visiting England most summers I never had the opportunity to experience the energy of a crop formation at first hand. In late summer 2008, I decided to devote some effort to finding a formation that I could enter. I spent several days driving around the southern counties and asking people for information on crop circles. Most of the people I met wanted to believe that all the formations that had appeared had been made by two old men with boards on their feet. They didn't want to know that one of the old men had died, that the formations were too complex to be made by humans and that they were appearing all over the world. It was apparent that for the people I met the thought of messages coming from sentient beings in other dimensions was very disturbing – yet I expect that some of the same people went to church and gladly heard about Angels appearing to shepherds with messages. This seemed to be a case of, "Not in my back yard!"

One day I was at the summit of Butser Hill, one of the highest points in the county of Hampshire. I had been scanning the surrounding countryside but could not find one crop formation. So I got out my pendulum and alphanumeric chart and asked my Guides. Their reply was that it was not yet time for that experience, but it was coming close.

Treasure Hunt

This year, 2009, as this book neared completion I had a different feeling about the crop formations. I felt that the time was coming for me to experience one at first hand. In early August I left for the UK armed with web sites reporting locations of crop circles, e.g., (Ref. 8-3). From the Internet I found that a likely area to explore was the vicinity of Avebury – the Wiltshire village set in a prehistoric stone circle. My Guides confirmed that the event was close and they recommended I start at Silbury Hill – a prehistoric earth works that looked like a conical pyramid, Figure 8-1.

One sunny morning in mid-August I arrived by car at Silbury Hill just before noon. As I loaded my backpack with a few supplies – and my pendulum – I noted with concern that the harvest was well under way. Would there be any fields of wheat still standing

174

to house a formation? I started my journey by attempting to climb Silbury Hill only to find access blocked by a fence erected by a local authority to 'protect the monument.' As I stood there wondering where to go the next 'clue' was presented to me – a helicopter flew low overhead and hovered over the crest of a nearby hill. I reasoned the occupants were photographing something interesting so I hiked to the top of the hill. From there I could see a formation in the distance but I 'knew' that one wasn't for me. Instead I recognized as my next clue a line of sarsen stones leading to the village of Avebury – that was where I had to go next. I hiked back to my car to drive to Avebury and enquire there.

So the treasure hunt unfolded for the next five hours; I would talk to people – like the kind folks in the Avebury 'Sarsen Shop'– who would direct me to the next point where I would talk to more people who would direct me further. I was told later in an Angel message (Appendix 8) that those people were put in my path to guide me to the crop formation called 'The Weave.' That was the name given to me by a young couple I met in a roadside parking place. As soon as I saw the astrology signs painted on the side of their van I knew they were the ones to ask. The young woman told me to walk over Milk Hill, which was in front of us, and as I passed the white horse I would see the formation called 'The Weave.'

It was close to 6:00 pm when I walked down Milk Hill and saw 'my' formation spread out before me. Figure 8-2 (Ref. 8-3) – the name 'The Weave' came from the interlaced squares in the design. Later, back in Vancouver, I found this formation was unusual in that it was created in three stages. The photo in Figure 8-2 was taken after the second stage. When I saw the formation, all three stages were complete, so that it looked much longer – it seemed to stretch away down the field for about a kilometer. Figure 8-3 (Ref. 8-3) shows the complete formation from a different angle.

My Crop Formation Experience

At last I had arrived! As I walked into the formation the first thing I noticed was that the farmer had put in the biggest circle a barrel with 'DONATIONS PLEASE' painted on the side. On top of the barrel was a locked steel box with a slot in the top. I put a two-pound coin in the box, glad that the farmer gave permission to enter his field in return for a donation.

I parked my backpack on the grass that was now growing between the bent wheat stalks – the formation was a few weeks old when I visited it. There was no other person in sight. I took out my pendulum and alphanumeric chart to contact my Guides and received a short message of congratulation on reaching this goal. I gave thanks to my Guides, to the Angels and All That Is for guiding me to this experience. I knew I had to complete it by meditating, which I did kneeling on the grass and bent wheat stalks with my eyes closed.

As I grew still I became aware of the gentle but vibrant energy of this place. I heard two sounds that seemed to surround me – a rasping sound like a wood stick being rubbed over another stick with notches cut in it and repeated high-pitched tones like an electronic triangle. I opened my eyes to check if anyone was near and could be responsible for the sounds but there was nobody in sight.

Weeks later, back in Vancouver, I was told that these sounds indicated the presence of Angels and while I had my eyes closed a ball of light came across the field, touched my heart and downloaded a message to my spirit. (This is another example of the effects I discussed in Chapter 4: Rings of Light.) But at the time I knew nothing of these things, only that I was elated at having reached an important goal in my life.

Back in Vancouver

About a month after my crop formation experience I was at home late at night reading a physics book about Zero Point Energy and some of Tesla's experiments (Ref. 8-4). I reached a section in the book about ball lightning both natural and artificial when suddenly I was overcome by a memory from my teenage years concerning a

176

ball lightning experience I had when I was a Royal Marine cadet on parade in a thunderstorm. I had not recalled this incident for many years but the memory was now so vivid it overwhelmed me.

I have learned to recognize such incidents as a device from my Guides for getting my attention, so I immediately contacted them through my pendulum. I asked them about the memory of the Royal Marine cadet parade in a thunderstorm. It seemed so remote from me that I thought I had imagined it so I asked if this event actually happened. My question brought a flood of answers:

Most definitely! A ball of lightning settled on your heart.
The boys around you were in awe of you.
You were touched by an Angel.
This event marked the start of your work.
Another Angel in a ball of light came to you in the crop formation.
This one had more information for you.
You will remember when you write again.

Atlantean Connection

The next morning I connected with my Guides and they told me to get my tape recorder operating, as I was going to channel the message that the Angel gave me in the crop formation. The total message I received is recorded as Appendix 8, but I will give the highlights as follows.

"This is the information we gave you as you knelt in that crop formation in the middle of the English countryside in Wiltshire near Silbury Hill which is a very important landmark for that area. It is a symbol of an earlier civilization that was partly responsible for the structures you know as Avebury and Stonehenge. In those days men still remembered the knowledge they had gathered at the time of Atlantis. Although in a scientific sense they were not as developed as you are now and certainly were not as developed as the original Atlanteans were, nevertheless they had very strong spiritual/scientific knowledge which they applied. As you know pyramids were very important in those days and we have talked to you about the tetrahedral structures in a pyramid that make it into a machine which can focus hyper-dimensional energy as you have so well written about in your previous chapters. Silbury Hill was a more recent version of a pyramid, more recent in the sense that it was since the time of Atlantis. But it was probably about the same time that pyramids were being built in Egypt that Silbury Hill was constructed."

"The people that lived in what you now call England were in communication with the people that lived in what is now called Egypt. In fact there was a worldwide connection between all these people. This was at a time of the recovery after the cataclysm that destroyed Atlantis when people started to recover from the great hardships they had endured. This was the time that led to the building of the second Atlantis on an island in the Atlantic near what you now call Gibraltar. This was a time of recovery, of remembering past knowledge and a time of rebuilding the Atlantean Empire but on a much more fundamental level. There was not the great ruling class and the magnetic temple of rejuvenation and all those very high flying scientific inventions that the Atlanteans had and used to their detriment. This new Atlantis was a much purer society that dealt with metals, in particular bronze. Bronze was made from copper (mixed with tin -MKS) brought from the area where the glaciers had retreated after the last ice age. You know about that source of copper (near the North American lakes -MKS) and how it was brought through Bimini to the new Atlantis. That led to what is now regarded as the Bronze Age."

"In that time there was a worldwide network formed by people who went out from the new Atlantis. Those people went to areas where their past life brothers had lived and were now living in new bodies but had not had the benefit of guidance in developing simple technologies connected with farming and subsistence living. Those people who came to help were regarded almost as gods by the people that received the information. That's where the names came from such as Kukulcan and Quetzacoatl that were applied the bearded white men that came from the second Atlantis and helped people who were struggling to return to some form of civilization. Those Atlanteans were connected with a worldwide network which understood the need for communication with other dimensions. They understood that their spiritual origins were in another dimension and they could receive energy from that dimension by constructing devices such as pyramids. That is why the pyramids were built in Egypt and why Silbury Hill was built in what is now Wiltshire."

"You were one of the Kukulcans that helped people understand about crops and creating craft objects like pottery and textiles. That is why you are so interested in that type of work in this lifetime. When you were young you used to help people in the technology network (for example people in third world countries -MKS) and you gave advice in making simple craft objects such as textiles and paper. – In that past lifetime you were part of the network that spread out first around the Atlantic and eventually the whole world. You traveled to Avebury so this lifetime's visits to places like Silbury Hill are certainly not the first; you have been there many, many times in other lifetimes."

"That was one of the reasons why we chose to guide you to the crop formation in that location, near Avebury for one thing, and the other thing that was significant was the crop formation had been given the name 'The Weave' which related to your connection with textiles and those skills which you imparted to more primitive people. You helped them come into a more craft oriented world where they had knowledge about farming, agriculture and cultivation and use of the materials made with those skills. That is the background to why that particular crop formation was selected for you."

"So all these things we have told you came to you while you were kneeling in that crop circle. We have explained the historical connections with that area and with that concept of the crop formation. While you were kneeling there all these ideas were implanted in your spirit. It came to you, if you are interested, in

179

a ball of light that traveled across the fields but you were not able to see that ball of light. It wasn't until the evening when you read a book that talked about ball lightening that you recalled that experience that you had in the Royal Marine cadets."

"We are happy that you knew what it was that you had to do when you set out that day to find a crop formation. We are very glad that you were persistent and were able to follow your intuition that guided you past those other crop formations that were on the horizon which you knew were not for you. We are pleased to see that you persisted in asking people where you had to go. Those people were put in your path to lead you to that crop formation called The Weave. Thank you for doing that and receiving this information from us."

The Message of the Crop Formation

The final version of the Milk Hill crop formation – as it became known on the Internet – is shown in Figure 8-3: As you can see by comparing Figures 8-2 and 8-3, the additional information takes the form of five lines of symbols. When I asked my Guides about those symbols they told me that they were Atlantean – the form used by people from the second Atlantis that brought about the Bronze Age and built Silbury Hill.

Intrigued by the strong Atlantean connections in this crop formation experience, I asked my Guides about it. They replied:

Glad you asked!
This formation was targeted specifically at ex-Atlanteans,
Those people will make a disproportionately large contribution to the new energy.
The new energy is the manifestation of All That Is on Earth.
Ex-Atlanteans will facilitate the spread of the new energy.
We are happy that you will be spreading the word with your book.

I was not surprised when my Guides offered to translate the five lines of symbols. When I saw the translation I realized this was

180

a fitting last item for my book. A message from Angels in hyper-dimensions giving us Guide Lines for living our physical lives on Earth.

Guides' Translation of Atlantean Message in Milk Hill Crop Formation

1   **Enter the temple of your body on Earth**

2   **Sing praise to All That Is for the gift of life**

3   **Take care of your beautiful planet**

4   **Be joyful in your work**

5   **Love is the greatest gift you can give each other**

References for Chapter 8

Ref. 8-1   *Circular Evidence* by Colin Andrews and Pat Delgado
Ref. 8-2   *Kryon Book 3 – Alchemy of the Human Spirit* by Lee Carroll
Ref. 8-3   www.cropcircleconnector.com
Ref. 8-4   *Tapping The Zero-Point Energy* by Moray B. King

The following pages give the appendices I have been quoting throughout the book.

The first is from my Guides and concerns zero point energy. All the rest are communications from the group of Angels called Crystal Light.

Appendix 1: Notes from Guides on Spiral Love Energy and Zero Point Energy

When I 'see' – with my eyes closed – energy leaving my body it is spinning counter-clockwise. It looks like a garden water sprinkler spinning out light instead of water. I asked my Guides about this and here is what they told me, but first I have to explain about zero point energy.

When atoms are cooled to absolute zero (-273 degrees Celsius) they should be still because all the energy has supposedly left them. But what is found is the atoms still jiggle around a bit – it seems they are bombarded by sub-atomic particles and this makes them move in random ways. This is called zero point energy (ZPE) which is explained in *The Field* by Lynne McTaggart (Ref. 2-3). Quantum scientists are realizing that the ZPE is the basis of inertia – why heavy things are difficult to move. My Guides tell me that spiral love energy – hyper-dimensional energy that is stepped down in intensity – unbalances the ZPE. They say:

The energy comes through the double star Sirius.
It devolves through strange loops.
It interacts with the zero point energy.
The ZPE is the working fluid for the spiral energy.

I asked, "Is this analogous to water being the working fluid for heat energy in a steam engine?" They replied:

That is a good analogy.

Then they continued:

Bias is introduced into the ZPE.
It means the inertia is less in a counter-clockwise direction.

I asked how humans use this energy and their reply was:

Humans go with the flow.
Their energy flows in a counter-clockwise direction as seen from above.

I asked where humans are directing this energy and they replied:

To all their creations.
All human works of art contain counter-clockwise spiral energy.
Also when we send you energy it leaves us counter-clockwise.
That is why your pendulum is entrained in a clockwise spiral for 'yes.'

The spiral energy of creation is discussed in Chapter 7.

Appendix 2: Angel Communication, May 1, 2008

We greet you Malcolm, enlightened one. You are our faithful helper and one of our brothers from past times. You sat in the seats of the explorers many times and came to all the sessions preparing you for this present adventure on Earth. The one you have so faithfully invested with your time and which you know is the most important activity in your life at this time.

We want to tell you about our realm that we inhabit, or occupy would perhaps be a better word. There is a dimension that you refer to as 5 and another that you would call 6. We are in both of these dimensions and between them. Our name is Angel, although a few of us have been in this position for ever and those are referred to as Archangels. We Angels have been many things on many planets but none of us has ever had a lifetime, or any time, living on Earth although we make many visits to your four dimensions and bring help to humans who have need of it.

We live in a kind of mist of physical energy which is not matter but is in a state about to become matter. So you would say, from your book definitions, we are partly condensed energy. This was the state human souls were in before they came to Earth and became physical, i.e., their energy completely condensed according to A. Einstein's equation although that applies only to the condensation of energy on the Earth plane.

We are in this semi-condensed form so that we are recognizable to our fellows and to some humans who can see us at certain times such as the announcement of the birth of Jesus to the shepherds. Those worthy men could see us just for the short time of the announcement. Come All Ye Faithful has been the hymn that humans have composed to commemorate that event and it gives a sense of the joy that was felt by all the people connected with that event.

Now we wish to tell you that we are not organized into choirs and different ranks such as Seraphim and all the categories that humans have put us in. Instead we have specializations in purpose as you have seen in your chart of the duties of the Archangels. We Angels are connected with one of those specializations, or in some cases with two or three of them. You will see what we mean if you look at your chart that you constructed from our words given in the 'Standing Stones Speak.'

Now we tell you how we interact with humans. Some of us do not have specific humans associated with us, but those Angels in that state are in a minority. Those Angels act as messengers interacting with any humans and beings on other planets, what you would call extra-terrestrials. Those free-of-human-responsibility Angels frequently accompany UFOs that provide the crop circle energy stamps. It is part of those Angels' duties to provide energy backup for the energy stamps.

However, the majority of Angels are associated with individual humans. And as you already know from your talk, 'Angels and Guides', each of us is responsible for two or three humans (sometimes as many as seven) which you call aspects. In that role you humans have called us Angels oversouls and it seems to convey a good sense of meaning so we are happy to use that term.

You are quite right in your description of the oversoul and human aspect. Indeed the humans are truly aspects, i.e., certain dimensional viewpoints = projections of our energy into the four dimensions that you occupy. So truly you are a special 'view' of our energy. By that last phrase we mean for example, Malcolm is a projection of Mikael's energy into the four dimensions of the Earth plane. Mikael has two other projections of himself in the Earth plane, one in England and one in Scandinavia.

It is best, for considerations of energy, if the different aspects of one Angel do not meet on the Earth plane. Although we let such a meeting almost occur between you and your 'brother' aspect in

188

a railway station in Holland so that you would see and recognize someone of identical energy, i.e., your aspect brother. This was a special event allowed because you were about to start writing your book. However, you and your aspect brother knew that you must not meet and speak to each other or energy difficulties would arise.

As you rightly say in your talk (which by now you must realize was a precursor to this revelation) aspects can share experiences with their sibling aspects. That is why several of you can lay claim to being some famous person in a past life. You have experienced Lavoisier's life and death through an aspect brother's experience while you were Erasmus Darwin.

Enough on aspects, we were just confirming the information given to you earlier and which you applied correctly in your talk.

Now in completion of this conveying of information to you, we want to talk about the guardian Angel role that we all play. It is our duty to look after all our aspects and we do this by watching them at all times. This can become an amusing scene, as Jane Roberts writes about, if an Angel is inexperienced in watching over his/her aspects. But in most cases we have had enough experience to be able to keep up with our responsibilities in this regard.

So if any of our aspects fell into some danger that is not on their path to experience then we help them avoid it, sometimes by apparently miraculous intervention. Such are the stories which humans like to tell about guardian Angels and their blessings.

In your case Malcolm, Michael has many times helped you drive past trucks safely although you were experiencing driving phobia. In the life threatening experiences you had, you know the three, your Angel Michael cooperated with your Guides of that time to bring you safely through the event. These events are typical of protection by guardian Angels which are the same being as that you call oversoul or higher self.

Now we bring this conveying of information to an end. Thank you for listening and writing so well. We are joyful that you are able to receive this information and can convey it to your fellow humans that will listen.

We give you all the blessings that are ours to give and we will continue to help you in your service to your fellow humans.

Malcolm K. Smith / May 1, 2008

Appendix 3: Angel Communication, April 24, 2009

Thank you dear Malcolm for agreeing to do this again. We are very happy that you are able to receive these messages from us in this way. We think that you will be very happy too with the results that you receive because there will be among the words we give you many new concepts about spiral energy in the universe.

Let us start with the source of this spiral energy. As your Guides started to tell you, in this galaxy that you call the Milky Way is one of the central stars that emit energy, the star that you call the Dog Star, Sirius. It has several cooperating stars dotted around the galaxy in the shape of a tetrahedron – would you believe? The stars are at the points of the tetrahedron and so you can work out how many stars there are acting as sources of this spiral energy. The energy comes from the source of all energy in the universe, what you refer to as God. We call that 'All That Is,' we know that you do as well Malcolm. This is the great presence that has made the universe and all the dimensions for the use of all the beings on the planets surrounding the stars in all galaxies. And those stars are present in the galaxy to feed the love energy out into their part of the galaxy. Your source of love energy from All That Is is the double star you call Sirius.

Because the energy that comes from Sirius is at such a high level of intensity it is necessary for that energy to be stepped down in intensity before it comes to your solar system. That is when a chain of what you call strange loops acts as a step-down transformer to bring the power down to levels acceptable to the beings on the planets in your area of the galaxy. Jacob saw a ladder leading into Heaven and Angels ascending and descending that ladder. He was seeing that same series of strange loops that you have modeled in wood and paper, but on a very limited scale of course. But you understand the concept of energy traveling around that loop until it becomes aware of itself. When it becomes aware of itself it moves into the next level, and so on up the ladder. The energy that comes from All That Is through the double star Sirius devolves down the ladder following the same path.

That path leads eventually to the sun, your local sun that you call Sun, in the centre of the solar system. It passes through the sun as if it were a window, and in fact it is exactly that, a window from the higher dimensions – that now you are beginning to call hyper-dimensions after Richard Hoagland's revelations. Those other dimensions encompass us, the Angels, and civilizations of beings on different planets that have learned to travel through some of those hyper-dimensions. Your Earth story that you call Star-Trek has fantasized about traveling from one part of the galaxy to another via the hyper-dimensions. This is done routinely by many civilizations around the galaxy. In due course so will the people of Earth that at the moment are working in the universe that you see in your four dimensions that you call space-time continuum.

The sun at the centre of your planetary system acts as a window in the veil between the hyper-dimensions and your space-time continuum and feeds this love energy at a stepped down acceptable level of intensity into your solar system. The amount of energy that comes through that window depends to a certain extent on where in the galaxy your solar system is situated because it revolves around the star Sirius in a long orbit. We are talking about your whole solar system revolving around Sirius in an orbit. Depending on where you are in that galactic orbit so the amount of radiation that comes from your sun changes. You could say it is like the summer and winter of your galactic travels.

In addition to solar energy which you perceive as sunlight there are other forms of energy that come to your planet. These also come through the sun but are not seen as electromagnetic radiation that affects your eyes so you are less aware of them although you are aware of them in some respects. Principally there is a force that you call magnetic which comes to the Earth through the sun from Sirius. As your scientists rightly guessed, magnetic energy is a form of hyper-dimensional energy. It comes from the hyper-dimensions through the sun just like sun light. When you wrote yesterday about an electric generator using electrons as a working fluid you were quite correct. The energy that is fed into your electrical systems in different countries of your earth comes from two sources.

As you tell the children in your science workshops, one source is the sun light which creates potential energy by placing water in high places so that when it is fed into a turbine it creates the spin that is necessary to rotate your generator armature. But that is only part of the energy and we would say that is a relatively minor part. The major part of the energy that is fed into the electrical systems of your planet comes from the hyper-dimensions in the form of magnetism which is the force that drives the electrons around the circuits creating the energy you regard as electricity.

That magnetic energy is available to you at all times and is not only critical for generating electricity but, as you have been told by Kryon, it is necessary to operate your living systems because your DNA and all the workings of your cells are attuned to a constant supply of magnetic energy. It is as if the DNA in your cells was constantly bathed in magnetic energy and from this is derived the energy of life or consciousness. It is a special gift to you from All That Is.

As you know these bodies that we talk about are just vehicles. For you are just like us, beings that exist independently of everything and revel in the Love that pours forth from All That Is. We sometimes reduce our energy level so that we can occupy a body and become a human or any one of the other hundreds of thousands of kinds of beings that are on all the planets in all the galaxies of the universe. There are unimaginable numbers of them.

Hoagland has correctly pointed out that it is not only the sun that sends energy from hyper-dimensions into the solar system. The planets receive energy from the hyper-dimensions because they too are rotating and they have at their centre a tetrahedron that issues energy out from the planet. That is why you read that several of the planets emit more energy than they receive from the sun. So it is not just a question of energy being reflected, for example by Neptune, but rather added to that reflected energy from the sun is energy that comes from the interior of the planet which nourishes the planet. Excess energy is sent out into the solar system and you people in the world experience this energy particularly when you consider astrology and the effects of the planets. The astrological influences that come to you on the planet Earth are the results of energy emitted by the planets. That energy that is emitted by the planets comes from their interior windows to the hyper-dimensions.

That energy of the planets that you perceive on Earth has creative energy. You, Malcolm, have been thinking about this a lot recently in connection with your book and this is what we want to devote the rest of this communication to. We are going to tell you how the energy that comes from the planets reaches Earth in the form of spirals. You experience it as spiral energy because as Hoagland so correctly says, "Everything is rotation, rotation, rotation." All the planets, the suns, the stars and the galaxies are rotating. So that energy that comes from any of those sources is seen to spin down to your planet's surface in the form of spirals.

As your Guides have told you those spirals have definite wavelengths and frequencies which characterize the energies. You on Earth are used to receiving these and feeling good, or not so good, depending on the frequencies of those energies. You have around you that great Cosmic Lattice that Kryon talks about. That is the storehouse of all those spiral energies. Humans have learned to reach out to that spiral energy in the Cosmic Lattice, which is also known as the 'Field' and 'Library of Knowledge' and by several other names as well. You know of which we speak. That energy is stored around you in a crystalline lattice.

Each cell of the lattice contains a considerable amount of energy which you can learn to release and use for various activities on Earth not the least of which is your creation of your day to day existence. That is why in the last few years it has become fashionable – and we

194

are very pleased to see this – to realize that humans create their own reality. The Law of Attraction, and other variations of that same philosophy, all tell you that in order to get a good result in your life it is necessary to approach your life with high hopes. In a good spirit you would say.

In your bodies you have a quantum field – which you defined correctly yesterday – a quantum field of photons which resonate together to form a standing wave of quantum possibility. From this you send out feelers to the lattice to make connections with it. The frequency of the feelers you send out is determined by your attitude, your mood. If you are in an upbeat mood then you have a particular type of frequency which we will refer to as 'good,' although it is not meant to have a value judgment on it. It's just a convenient label to distinguish it from low expectations, which we will call 'bad' frequencies. If you have a good frequency then you resonate with the cells in the matrix that have that kind of energy and what you regard as good energy – good fortune – comes to you in your everyday lives. That is the process by which people create their own realities.

On the other side of the coin is the situation in which you have a miserable attitude and you expect bad things to happen then you will connect with those cells in the lattice that have those low levels of energy that you are looking for. More low energy will be fed back to you by the resonance process. That will lead to apparently bad things happening in your life but, of course, all this is part of your experience. When you decided to come to planet Earth these were the things that you decided to experience and this is the mechanism of that experience. You can experience what you call good and bad by the way you approach the lattice, resonate with it and receive energy from it.

For an artist, anyone doing creative work, which of course includes creative scientists like you, you will know that there are certain parts of the lattice where you can get the energy that you need. Because that energy that comes from All That Is is full of creative potential and artists, inventors and musicians, people who are creative, know where to go on the lattice to receive that creative potential as part of the spiral energy.

In every painting you see, in every invention you have, in every piece of music you hear there is spiral energy. In the music that shows up as strange loops, that is the most apparent illustration of the strange loop characteristics of the spiral energy. For artists and inventors the loop structure of the energy is less obvious. Nevertheless it is there, and you Malcolm are beginning to understand about that spiral energy that is occurring in paintings. Your friend Michelle is also aware of that energy too and you can together identify that energy by processes which you will discover as you go into the work which you are preparing to write about in the next chapter of the book you are writing.

You have made a good start with your theory of abstraction which looks at the structure of pictures in a spiral scanning way and measures the energy response of the painting. You have made the realization that variation in the energy response of the painting is an important measure of quality of the painting and its impact on people. Humans prefer pictures that give them the most variation in the energy response of the painting from angle to angle to angle as you scan around the painting. In your theory of abstraction you have perceived that quality of paintings so we encourage you to follow up on that.

That is all we wanted to tell you at this time, but you will receive more details particularly about the creative spiral energy and its relationship to pictures, music and inventions when you are writing your chapter. That information will come via your Guides. They will give you detailed knowledge in those areas. What we wanted to do today was to give you a broad overview of the whole process as it devolves down from All That Is.

Thank you for communicating with us and for making it possible for us to bring these ideas into your physical world. We are very happy that you are engaged on this research and your writing. We will help you in every way we can. Now we leave with all the blessings that are ours to give and much love to you Malcolm and to all your co-workers in this great adventure.

Malcolm K. Smith / 26 April, 2009

Appendix 4: Angel Communication, May 6, 2009

Hello Malcolm. Well done, you have responded to this very quickly and very readily. We are very happy that you can do this for us again. We think you will be happy with the results because they relate to your book and the information that you need to continue your book and to have a full record of all the aspects of the energy that comes from hyper-dimensions. We are watching you write and preparing to write and we see that you still have some areas where there is uncertainty. We are pleased to see that you experiment with diagrams trying to understand how the tetrahedron is involved with the spiral energy. Why the tetrahedron shape – like pyramids (which are double tetrahedrons -MKS) – is important. Why the tetrahedron is important inside planets and how that relates to the spiral energy that comes from them. So it is with that in mind that we come to you today to talk about that and to enlarge on what it is that you need to know about that process.

The facets of each tetrahedron, each of the faces of the tetrahedrons, are in the form of triangles as you know. These triangles intersect with spirals along which the energy from hyper-dimensions is vibrating. These vibrations run along the spirals so they are longitudinal waves, or pulses you could call them, pulses of greater and lesser intensity in the form of a wave going past any particular point. That kind of radiation comes into a triangle and is picked up by the triangle like an antenna. The triangle sees, in terms of physics, or experiences the changes in the intensity of the energy in the form of a wave and this wave is picked by the facets of the tetrahedrons acting like antennae. When you are doodling on some paper draw some triangles and some spiral wave forms (or make models -MKS) and you will see that, whatever the wavelength is, there is some part of the triangle in which the sides are at the right separation to resonate with each part of the wave. So the triangle is a universal antenna for any waves of energy that are coming in – whatever the wavelength the triangles that form the tetrahedrons can pick them up and focus them.

Whatever the material is that they are made of, be it glass, stone or metal, the tetrahedrons refract the energy waves that come from the hyper-dimensions. Like light being refracted by a glass of water – as you show the children making the straw look bent – in this case the energy travels more slowly as it enters the material of the tetrahedron and so it is refracted into the interior of the tetrahedron. There is always some separation of the sides of the triangle which fits the wave perfectly and allows that refraction to take place completely. So the tetrahedron acts as an ideal lens – although strictly speaking it is not a lens – for the spiral energy waves that come from the hyper-dimensions. As a result the tetrahedrons draw into their interior most of the energy that is in their path.

So the bigger the tetrahedron the greater is the amount of energy that can be gathered. Really small tetrahedrons – like the small pyramidal devices that people make to collect energy and retransmit it – can pick up small amounts of energy. Of course, really large tetrahedrons like the actual pyramids can pick up much larger amounts of energy. It does not matter whether the pyramid has smooth sides or steps, the same process works in each case. So the Mayan step pyramids are just as effective at gathering hyper-dimensional energy as are the Egyptian pyramids. Of course in the Egyptian pyramids it is known that the focus, of the lens as we could call it, of the tetrahedrons of the pyramid is what you normally call the King's Chamber. But this is a misnomer because it was never intended that the king or pharaoh would have his body put there. Instead it was a place where people like the pharaoh and other people of high standing in the Egyptian society could go and receive energy from hyper-dimensions. As a result they could go out of body and experience other dimensions through the energy that was beamed into them at that focus called the King's Chamber.

As we told you last time the energy that comes from All That Is through Sirius is stepped down as it comes through your sun at the centre of your solar system. It comes through your sun like a window. That energy also comes through all the planets in the solar system. All those energies from the sun and all the planets come

200

to your Earth and are available for picking up by tetrahedrons. The Egyptians, the Mayans, and the Atlanteans and Lumurians before them, knew about this energy and that is why pyramids are such an important part of their societies. They realized that these buildings or devices could act as lenses and focus the hyper-dimensional energy for the benefit of the people in those societies.

Of course that is why you are beginning to know about the pyramids on Mars, because those societies of Atlantis and Lemuria, and others before that, had prior existence on the fourth planet out from the sun which you call Mars. They already knew when they lived on Mars that the hyper-dimensional energy could be gathered in that way. That is why those tetrahedral structures were assembled on Mars. As Richard Hoagland has correctly suggested there is a very strong connection between the society that existed on Mars and the society that you call Egypt. The face on Mars and the Sphinx of Egypt both originate from the same society and historical concepts that were carried from Mars to Earth by Spirit. That is of historical interest and support for Richard Hoagland's theories. We will not go into that any more at this time.

Now we want to talk about another aspect of the tetrahedral structures around you. We have talked about the pyramids and, of course, you know that each planet has within it the double tetrahedron which has its points against the outer surface of the planet at what you would call 19.5 degrees north or south of the equator. This is a fact of geometry and is not variable with different planets. Richard Hoagland has said quite correctly that these tetrahedrons inside the planets issue forth energy. They receive the energy from Sirius. It is picked up by the tetrahedral lenses inscribed inside each planet and it issues forth from the planet's surface. On occasions there is visual evidence of this such as the great red spot on Jupiter. Hoagland has talked about this at length and he is quite correct about maintenance of that spot for many millennia, although humans have only observed it for about 300 years. However, that is enough to give your scientists pause in explaining the stability of that apparent storm on the surface of Jupiter.

The planets have within them a double tetrahedron that receives the energy from Sirius and transmits it into the solar system. We talked last time about the energy radiated from the outer planets being greater than the energy they receive from the sun. This is good evidence that more energy is coming internally through the planet and is radiating out into the solar system. As an aside we say this is the basis of astrology and the influence of the planets on the lives of conscious beings such as humans on Earth.

We talked about the double tetrahedrons in the planets as a refresher of what we said last time. (April 24, 2009 -MKS) Also this is an introduction to a double tetrahedron which is much more applicable to humans. Of course we are talking about the double tetrahedron structure of the merkaba, or energy body, which is around every human. Those energy structures have been drawn and modeled by Drunvalo Melchizedek and he has explained in great detail those tetrahedral structures, which are themselves made of energy existing around the human body. Of course, you can't see those structures until you become attuned to focusing on that particular form of energy. The energy that is used to construct the merkaba around humans is similar in characteristics to the energy that is beaming in from the sun and planets into your Earth plane and is picked up by humans.

As soon as humans give intent to live a spiritual life, following the examples and instructions set up by Kryon, then they receive a merkaba around their bodies. It is quite small to start with but it is constructed from energy that has come from the sun and planets in the form of a spiral. Once a person has received a merkaba, and realized that they have it, then they can absorb more energy using it because the double tetrahedral structure of the merkaba acts as a lens to bring in more spiral energy as it comes from the sun and planets. Once the energy tetrahedrons have been set up around a human, that makes it possible for the human to gather more energy and to grow their tetrahedral structure to an enormous size. In your Earth measurements you would say that from one side to another is of the order of 50 feet in a very well developed merkaba. Yours

202

Malcolm is of the order of 25 feet. You are doing very well but you are at the beginning of this process of absorbing energy. The more you understand about this the more energy you will absorb, the greater will become your merkaba and therefore the more energy that it can absorb. So it increases in an exponential way once you start that process of growing your merkaba.

This is an important process for all humans but sadly to say there are relatively few that are even prepared to think about such things. While it is not necessary for them to consciously run this process in their lives it is necessary for them to give some attention to spiritual matters. There are relatively few humans on the planet Earth who at the present time give any thought to spiritual matters. That is one of the reasons why we bring you this information. We want you to put in your book all the things that we have given you because we want you to influence more people to understand that if they just give some attention – we are not saying that they have to give all their attention, or even half of it, but some significant part. If they would think about spiritual matters a little bit each day, for example by saying a few prayers or being concerned about the welfare of their fellow humans, then they will receive a merkaba. If they will give intent to lead a spiritual life as Kryon says they will start to grow a merkaba which once it's started will continue to grow feeding on the energy that's coming from Sirius via your sun and planets.

This is why we want you to talk about these things. To make people realize how much of the strange phenomena that you see around that people on Earth talk about is based on the energy that is coming from Sirius by those pathways that we just told you. There are many factors that influence it and you have already covered some of those in the first chapters of your book. For example, you talk about the crop circles and those are obvious, we think, obvious messages for humans to consider. But even in that case there are many people who don't want to think about such strange things and would rather shut their minds to those events, those artifacts that they see around them. So they shut themselves off from a valuable source of energy which could increase their consciousness levels greatly.

We refer to the man who wrote the book, *Power Versus Force* (David Hawkins -MKS). He has many years ago given intent to lead a spiritual life and help other people. As a result he has grown a large merkaba and the information that has been fed to him has been on the increase of consciousness of the human race. He has written how the growth of one person's consciousness can compensate for many people who do not grow their consciousness. This man has helped many people with this understanding and we are very grateful to him for explaining this to his fellow humans. But once again relatively few people are prepared to listen to his views and suggestions. Once we can get people to read the book then they see that this is an explanation of events that are going on in the world around them.

There have been many events in the past that people thought were exciting and wonderful, for example meetings with extra-terrestrial beings and in some cases extra–dimensional beings, like ourselves the Angels. Unfortunately, many people when they receive these connections or experiences just revel in the strangeness of it – what you would call the 'gee-whiz' reaction – and they can't wait to tell their friends about it. But they don't see that this is a demonstration of spiritual things happening around them. We are not saying that all inter-planetary beings are very spiritual, there are some that have what you would call negative attitudes. But generally speaking most of the inter-planetary beings that your race comes into some sort of contact with are beneficial and want to help you understand the greater structure of the universe and the energy that's available to all of you both personally and in the form of devices from which you can gather energy for your physical tasks.

You have been talking today in the schools about generating electricity. We told you last time that we spoke like this that much of the energy that is moving the electrons along a wire comes via the magnetic field and of course that magnetic energy is an inter-dimensional force. It's not the same in quality as the hyper-dimensional energy that we have just been talking about. Nevertheless it is hyper-dimensional. Electromagnetism is a lower form of energy but it is very useful for humans and for many, many races around the universe to use. This is another gift from All That Is. When you create electricity in your society you are using part of the energy that comes from higher dimensions. But this is a separate class of energy, we would call it, that is not of the same intensity as the energy that you call hyper-dimensional.

You have written earlier about love energy. Your Guides helped you find the frequency of that love energy. It was a very high number – 10^{33} – as far as we recall, and that is about the change-over point from electromagnetic energy which is at that frequency and lower. The electromagnetic energy changes over to being, what you call, hyper-dimensional energy at around that frequency. Above that frequency is pure love energy. You can view that cut off as being 10^{33}, above that is considered love energy, below that is electromagnetic energy. When Hoagland and people like that talk about hyper-dimensional energy coming through the sun and planets they are referring to spiral energy which comes at a frequency of 10^{33} and higher.

Another characteristic of that love energy is that it is in the form of a spiral whereas the electromagnetic energy has some spiral characteristics but is mostly in the form of a wave in one or two dimensions. Energy characteristics will be explained later. It is just necessary for you to understand that there are differences. All this energy is available for humans to use either in electromagnetic form or in the hyper-dimensional form. Your society can learn to capture the hyper-dimensional energy and use it in ways that will benefit all the planet. Already people are using electromagnetic energy in that way and those methods have been suppressed by concerns on the Earth that already have a good grip on the limited energy supplies of the planet. Those powerful forces tend to suppress any new forms of free energy because they won't make any money from it. But that situation is not going to last much longer with the new energy that is coming to the planet. The days of those energy pirates will soon be over and natural methods to gather electromagnetic and hyper-dimensional or spiral energy will become harvested from the stars and used in your future societies.

You Malcolm can make a good contribution to this by explaining in your book about the availability of these energy forms. We think you had better add in retrospect that when we talk about hyper-dimensional energy we are referring to spiral energy as opposed to electromagnetic energy which is basically in a wave form and is a slightly simpler form of energy. Another even simpler form of energy is gravitation which is basically an inertial effect. You can understand about that from the book *The Field*.

You have magazines that talk about ways of measuring some of these energy forms. When you saw in Hoagland's DVD about the torsional pendulum you felt a start of recognition that is because in previous lifetimes you have used that kind of device to measure energies. You should consider building another one again and using it to detect subtle energies in various situations such as coming from your body, coming from works of art and other similar sources. For sure you will find a lot of experimentation you can do with the torsional pendulum. I think you remember you encountered this device many years ago when you were a research chemist and you wanted to measure properties of fibers with a very small torsional pendulum. You were quite keen to do that at that time and that was because you anticipated the need for something like this as you got older and became engaged in this work. In a similar way when you were young you anticipated the need for the theory of abstraction which talks about how that energy is encoded in pictures, particularly works of art. So you have had foreshadowing of this work that is now coming to you Malcolm. You are not surprised when you hear these terms like 'torsional pendulum' and 'mechanism of abstraction' because you know that those ideas were given to you to prepare you for work you would do later in life.

All these things will be explained in later books that you will write. For now we want you to just talk about the different forms of energy and how they interact with tetrahedral structures. That is the main point of our discussion today. We will not take up more of your time. We would like you to write this material down so you have a record of it and can show it to other people. You can include it as part of your book if you wish. We are sure this material will help you in writing your chapters and explaining these effects to other people, particularly the chapter you have just started on which talks

206

about where the energy comes from. This is a good basis for that chapter.

Thank you Malcolm for taking this time to record our words. We are very pleased that you are so ready to pick up your recorder and talk for us when your Guides ask you to. That is a valuable response that you achieve that way and we are sure that the rewards that come from that will please you and make it well worth you spending this time with us and recording our words. We appreciate the help you give us and your fellow humans by doing this work and we will come to you again with more information at a later time.

Now we leave you and send you all our blessings. We hope you have a happy evening working on these words that we have given you already. Thank you Malcolm and good night.

Malcolm K. Smith / 10 May, 2009

Appendix 5: Angel Communication, May 14, 2009

Thank you, Malcolm for overcoming difficulties and making it possible for us to communicate again like this. We appreciate your efforts in getting everything running smoothly and the roadblocks out of the way. We want to tell you some more information today about how things work in connection with the hyper-dimensional forces. This is the third of our – we will call them lessons – in the physics of hyper-dimensional forces. You have done very well to record all those words on paper. Now we want to talk about the way planets like Earth form a matrix around them. You see that matrix as a web of hexagonal cells. You saw a picture in Drunvalo Melchizadek's book in which there was a web of hexagonal cells around a galaxy. This is part of a scientist's theory which is described in National Geographic Magazine 1979. If you look in the index for that year you will find a reference to a web of cells being theorized by Earth physicists to be around a galaxy. This is something that comes out of the equations when energy is seen to flow from stars in a galaxy – like your star Sirius which is your closest hyper-dimensional energy emitting star.

As we told you before, that star you call Sirius sends information and energy from hyper-dimensions into your solar system through your local sun and planets. That energy from Sirius, and the other hyper-dimensional energy emitting stars in your galaxy forms a boundary layer around the outside of your galaxy. That is a point where the energy that is emitted by the stars in the galaxy reaches a limit and curls back inside. When it does that is when that hexagonal form lattice is produced. The same kind of lattice occurs around your sun and planets.

You remember we told you that the hyper-dimensional energy that comes from Sirius is emitted by the sun and planets in your solar system. Some of that energy when it reaches the outer limits of the planet doubles back on itself and is reabsorbed for the use of the planet. The energy comes out of the points where the double tetrahedron touches the inner surface of the planet – as evidenced by the great red spot on Jupiter. That energy is emitted through all those tetrahedral touching points from the planet and could be lost to the planet because it tends to radiate out into space for the benefit of other planets. Each planet receives a contribution of that energy from all the other planets and the sun. But at the same time each planet needs some of its emitted energy for its own use, its own well being. So some of the energy that is emitted by the tetrahedral touching points is absorbed back into the planet's surface and that is where the hexagonal structures are formed.

You will find, Malcolm, that there is evidence of structures like this on some of the planets. If you check through the Hoagland book again you will see an example of a hexagonal structure lattice being seen on one of the planets in the outer part of your solar system. Because there is just one planet described as having this structure does not mean that the other planets do not have it; in fact it is around every planet. Some of the energy emitted by each planet is absorbed back into the planet and takes the form of a hexagonal lattice. There is a hexagonal matrix of energy hovering just above the surface of the planet.

Of course Earth is no exception to this. Earth sends out from the tetrahedral touching points hyper-dimensional energy which it has received internally from Sirius. That energy radiates out into space but a portion of it curls back so that it forms a hexagonal structure lattice around the Earth. In the hexagonal structure lattice or matrix is stored a great deal of energy and a lot information which the humans on Earth can access. This is what Kryon refers to as the Cosmic Lattice and others have referred to it as the 'Field.' Gregg Braden calls it the 'Divine Matrix.' All those descriptions are of the same thing. It is a web of information, of knowing and a web of energy.

The energy comes from within the planet and is projected out through tetrahedral touching points inside the planet's surface and the energy forms this hexagonal lattice. But at the same time information comes to that lattice as well. Part of it comes through the centre of the Earth by the same route as the hyper-dimensional energy and part of the information is contributed by the people of Earth. All the humans that have had lifetimes on Earth leave their collected wisdom, understanding and learning and it is deposited in the hexagonal lattice structure. This is what is referred to as the Web of Knowing, the Collective Unconscious or the Akashic Record. It is a depository of the information that has been gathered in all the lifetimes of all the humans that have lived on the Earth. There is a great deal of information that has been gathered and stored there.

All the information in the lattice and all the energy in the lattice is available to all the humans who have a lifetime on Earth at present. They can resonate with different parts of the lattice and from it they can obtain energy which the humans can then use to create their futures. They can also obtain information from the lattice to help solve problems or develop new things for the Earth. This is what you refer to, in your creativity talk, as inspiration; the knowledge from the lattice is 'breathed in,' hence the word inspiration. It becomes part of the human, the human resonates its personal quantum field with the information residing in the cosmic lattice.

In doing so the human partakes of that information, borrows it or uses it, but it does not lessen the sum total of the information in the lattice. You can think of the lattice as being like a library where humans can go and borrow a book – we are suggesting that is what they do when they resonate with part of the lattice – information comes to the human but at the same time the information stored in the library is not lessened by the resonation exchange with the human. So the information in the library remains at the level it was at before the human resonated with it. The lattice is not reduced in its power. In fact the opposite happens and as each human resonates with the lattice and receives information from it then the outcome of the human's spiritual processes – which you would probably think of as mental processes in creating something – is fed back to the lattice and adds to its sum total of knowledge.

The hexagonal lattice around your planet, and around any planet, works as a library of information. It is constantly interchanging information with the beings on the planet. The beings use that information and feed back the work they do to the lattice so that the sum total of the information held by the lattice increases as it is used. It is never diminished, but rather is augmented, by the use by the people that live on each planet.

We have told you about the Earth in this particular example. But any planet that has sentient beings on it works in the same way with its lattice and its interaction with the beings. Not only sentient beings – maybe what you would call thinking beings – but also apparently non-thinking beings like animals know about the lattice subconsciously, have a natural understanding of it and can draw on it for information necessary for their survival such as location of water and whatever sustenance they need. All that information is available to all the creatures that live on the planets.

When humans on planet Earth want to undertake some creative endeavor they resonate their quantum field, which you have already seen consists of standing waves of light within the energy structures they call their bodies. Humans have these energy structures that are quite similar between all humans – Peggy Dubro has drawn diagrams that we gave her that illustrate how those quantum fields appear in a semi-physical state. Although, of course, very few humans can actually see that quantum field, you can all be aware of it. Part of your giving intent is to develop your awareness of your quantum field and how you can resonate that with the lattice, the divine matrix or what ever you want to call it in order to obtain information to help you with your tasks that you have to do on the planet on which you live.

The matrix, which Kryon refers to as the cosmic lattice, is around your Earth in a physical sense but it is only faintly seen by some individual humans and only under certain circumstances. That is because the energy and information, which are essentially the same thing – you could call it information/energy – the two are just different forms of the same basic energy. That information/energy exists in several dimensions at one time. So the cosmic lattice should not be thought of as being a physical thing of your four-dimensional existence but rather it partially shows up in your four dimensions although it exists in all twelve dimensions of which the universe consists.

When a human wants to derive energy or information from the lattice then that person goes into an inter-dimensional connection with the lattice; goes into an inner space, you might call it, in order to resonate with the lattice. This is why it appears that inspiration comes to you from within your bodies because it is within your bodies that you form that resonating structure of your quantum field. You have the experience, the words that you say in your Western World, of going into inner space in order to resonate with the lattice and gain inspiration.

It appears to you humans that you are given ideas. You are not sure where those ideas come from, but many of you understand that it is a spiritual experience to receive that information. You give thanks for the information, for the ideas, for the inspiration. That thanks, that understanding of the nature of the gift facilitates further connections. We would say that the more gratitude you show for the information you receive, the energy you receive, the more you can receive that energy and inspiration. Your process of resonating with the lattice becomes exercised, becomes more proficient and you are able to seek just the right kind of inspiration that you need for your tasks. It is like exercising a muscle to make it stronger. In this case the 'muscle' we are referring to is your ability to resonate your quantum field with certain parts of the lattice in order to acquire energy from it or to acquire information from it. Those two things really are the same thing it is just that for humans it is more convenient to think of them as being two separate concepts.

Well, Malcolm, that is the total story of how the energy forms those hexagonal structures that have been glimpsed by scientists either in a practical or a theoretical situation. They've got their ideas about the hexagonal lattice from their own lattice. So you could say this is an example of the lattice informing people about its own existence.

That is a very good example of self-reference on which the strange loop ladders are based. The knowledge that comes to you knows that it exists and it is able to present itself whenever a human needs that information. The lattice is a self-regulating, self-perpetuating device that helps the beings of your planet. The same system is repeated for all the planets in the galaxy. So that inspiration is available to all from the cosmic lattice that is around each of the planets.

That is all we wanted to tell you today. This has been relatively quick once we got started so it should not take you long to transcribe this. We know you can learn a great deal from the transcription process. If there are other pieces of information that we have not conveyed to you today then we will convey those as you come to the relevant part of the transcription. Thank you Malcolm for making it possible to do this today especially in spite of your received negative road blocks. We are very pleased you were able to overcome those road blocks and receive our communication. We will help you explain all this in your book and explain it to the scientists. Thank you Malcolm for helping us convey these words to you today. We will do all we can to help you put all this into a good form as a record that can be part of your book.

Now we say good bye to you, we give you our blessings and send you our love. Until the next time that we talk again like this. Good bye.

Malcolm K. Smith / 16 May, 2009

Appendix 6: Angel Communication, June 8, 2009 (+ Guides' words)

Hello Dear Malcolm. We were glad to hear that you were able to get a new recorder which is more reliable than the previous one. We are happy to give you these messages again that we already gave two days ago. This time we want to talk about hyper-dimensional energy, but just that part of it which we will refer to as love energy. We want to talk about how it interacts with human biology.

As you know the hyper-dimensional energy is divided into three parts by the stepping down process and the lowest of these energy forms is gravity. The next highest is electromagnetism of which magnetism itself is a part. And the highest energy, with respect to frequency, is love energy. You have already seen that love energy is defined as electromagnetic energy at a frequency above 10^{33} hertz. Now we tell you about that love energy and how it comes into your body. What it does in your body too.

Malcolm you have often wondered, being a chemist, what is happening in your body to generate all those specific proteins that are necessary for example to build DNA. When you give your talks you tell people that there are only four different base compounds, adenine for example, that are needed for building DNA. And yet in your diet you may not have any of that material and obviously some of the proteins that you do eat in your food may need to be changed so that they are suitable for any particular physiological reaction in your body.

This is where the love energy comes in because by transforming energy into atoms the right kind of atoms can be generated at the reaction site so that the necessary molecules can be made from them. For example, if you had two carbon atoms available from something that you had eaten and you had lots of hydrogen and oxygen atoms available then the love energy would make more carbon atoms by transmuting the oxygen atoms. Those extra carbon atoms that had just been manifested by the addition of love energy to the oxygen atoms can then be used to build the necessary molecules that are required in that reaction and that particular area of your body.

The most important compounds that are doing these kinds of reactions are the enzymes. There are thousands of different enzymes in your body and each has a specific chemical reaction to facilitate. Part of that facilitation is assembling the right numbers of atoms to build the compound that the enzyme is specific for. If the enzyme has not got the right number of atoms to assemble into the required molecule it brings in love energy which manifests itself as the required atoms. Then those atoms can be built by the enzyme into the necessary molecule which in many cases is fitted into the still larger macromolecule needed in the body. The example we have been giving is the protein base materials that are fitted into the DNA chain.

It is fairly unlikely that the right materials will be available, to fit into the DNA chain as it grows, just from the raw materials that are present in the diet of the person. So it is necessary to modify the atoms in such a way that the required ones are available at the site of the building of the DNA molecule. As you tell in your talks, when the cells divide the double helix pair of DNA molecules zip apart like a zip fastener and one side of the zip fastener goes with the new cell and the other side remains with the parent cell. That means that a new single strand of DNA has to be built in each cell to complete the pair. Since that code is specific for that particular cell then a certain array of the four basic proteins is necessary to be assembled to continue replicating its DNA. Nature – God – has realized that it is highly unlikely that the necessary atoms are present in the required numbers to form whatever compounds are required and so it becomes necessary to manifest the required atoms. That is where love energy comes in and provides that requirement.

You see on a physical basis love energy has a critical function to perform. It also performs another critical function in a spiritual sense but we talk about that on another occasion in the part of your book on creativity when you talk about humans creating their futures. Once again love energy comes in and manifests various things that the humans give intent for. That is on a different scale to the manifesting of atoms and molecules that each human body requires. But in both cases love energy provides the required physical material. When we say physical material it is, after all, just collections of energy. It is a relatively simple thing for the love energy to configure itself in such a way that the required atoms can be manifested at the reaction site.

In this way it is essential that humans absorb love energy because they literally grow from that energy just as a plant needs the electromagnetic energy from the sun to build cellulose molecules so humans need love energy, also through the sun. That window in the hyper-dimensions, that you refer to as the sun, sends you the love energy that is required to build the proteins and other molecules that make up your bodies. So you are using not photosynthesis but energy synthesis just like a plant or tree.

When that energy comes into the parts of your body where the reaction is building the molecules the energy is gathered by tetrahedral arrangements of atoms. Just as the galaxy has a tetrahedral arrangement of energy stars, your pyramids and your human energy structures called merkabas have tetrahedral structures so on the scale of atoms tetrahedral structures are formed by carbon atoms too. You remember from your early chemistry knowledge at school and the first part of university that the valency directions of a carbon atom are in the edges of a tetrahedron. The angle between bonds of four hydrogen atoms attached to a carbon atom in the methane molecule is called a tetrahedral angle.

One of the reasons that carbon is chosen as the material that forms so much of your living matter on the planet Earth is that carbon atoms have bond directions with other atoms that form tetrahedral structures. Even in macromolecules where there is a carbon backbone, perhaps with hydrogen atoms attached, those bonds are all formed at tetrahedral angles. That makes it possible for love energy to be gathered because those tetrahedral angles act as antennae for the love energy as it flows through the bodies of the people who are growing as a result of that process. So you would probably call it a miracle that human life is based on carbon, and carbon has that critical valency angle associated with it that is necessary to receive love energy from the sun or the planets. This is something that has been devised by the Creator and you would probably say that it seems miraculous. It is miraculous that it all fits together so beautifully and it works without any problems whatsoever.

Now we think we have covered most of the material that we presented earlier (previous recording failed -MKS). We do not think it's necessary to continue talking about the chemistry as we would also tell you about other uses of love energy. Once the chemistry has been started and the human body is growing well, through chemistry the synthesis of necessary molecules continues unabated and unnoticed by the human. All that's known is the human has to eat nutritious foods and those get converted into body material.

At the same time the tetrahedral structures of the carbon atoms are absorbing energy and bringing more and more energy into the body. Not all of that love energy is needed to act as raw material for the synthesis of proteins and other molecules. Some of it is fed into the body and is used as energy by the body. There are two general energies circulating in the body which come from that love energy.

The first of these is the energy that your Asian people call 'Chi.' This is the energy of life. It is the energy that flows around the human body in the meridians and you know about this energy now from your people that do acupuncture. They use that Chi energy and channel it in a way to cure various diseases of the body. When they do that what is happening is the love energy is directed into the diseased part and the love energy can change the physical structure of the human body at that point. That is what happens when acupuncture is applied. It is quite miraculous to see the cures that result. But the mechanism of that miracle is that the Chi energy

– which is just another form of love energy – is channeled into particular areas of the body and changes in the physical structure of the body take place.

Sometimes it is not necessary for an acupuncture specialist to divert those Chi flows instead maybe the person can bring about the miracle themselves. You hear of miraculous cures at times and these come about because the person – through intent, through their faith – believes that they can cure themselves and the individual human being brings that love energy through the body to the point where it is needed. The enzymes, that we talked about, take over and from that energy manifest the required molecular structure in the area to bring about the necessary cure.

Bodies are able to repair themselves as long as they have a human spirit in them to give intent to cure the body. You have seen some miraculous films, videos and photographs of religious adepts in other cultures. For example, the Hindu culture where they can put metal rods through the flesh of their cheeks, their arms, their chests. They can manifest no pain and when they remove those metal rods the flesh is healed immediately. This is another example of love energy manifesting the required molecules at the point of the miraculous penetration and removal of the metal rods.

When those miraculous surgeons, of which there are many particularly in the Philippines and Brazil and all over the world, perform so called bloodless operations those people are operating with love energy. By directing it they are able to change the molecular structure of parts of the patient's body. They are cooperating with the body's enzyme systems to manifest flesh and blood at the points of repair and that is perceived as a cure by the patient.

That is very impressive because it is fast but on a lesser scale there are many healers who are able to receive Chi energy, which is love energy, and to direct it into the bodies of willing recipients. They change the molecular structure at the points in the body to which the energy is applied by the same process that we have been talking about – manifesting from the love energy the required physical molecules in the right configuration to provide a cure for the human body.

All those healing techniques depend on bringing in love energy and applying it so that the necessary molecules and structures of a healthy body are manifested from the energy. You see this pattern occurring many times. In a previous chapter of your book you talked about Angel energy being manipulated and solidified or condensed into matter manifesting, for example, miraculous pictures on a cloak or on a wall. All these miraculous things that you see are based on the same mechanism – that of love energy coming in and condensing into atoms, molecules and structures which are part of human bodies or pictures from which humans can receive a message. These miraculous cures are the great gift that our Heavenly Father, Heavenly Mother, All That Is sends to us. When adepts materialize objects from apparently nothing they are using the same technique of bringing that love energy in and creating a molecular structure which is perceived as the object that is manifested. This is the same reaction in all those situations and that is the great gift that is bestowed upon us all. In human situations it leads to actual physical manifestations from that love energy.

Now we think we have conveyed enough of this miracle for you, Malcolm, to be able to write about it. We are very pleased that you have a chemistry background from which you can talk about atoms, molecules and molecular structures quite comfortably. Did you realize when you were studying the structure of aminoanthraquinone molecules (My Ph.D. research -MKS) and how they absorb certain wavelengths of electromagnetic radiation – coloured light – that you would be one day writing about love energy being absorbed by tetrahedral structures of carbon atoms. It is because you are so familiar and comfortable dealing with chemical structures that you are able to receive this information and understand its significance. This was part of the preparation for you writing this book when you came to your second lifetime in the same body. We are very happy

220

that you have learned your chemistry lessons so well and are able to absorb this information and the beautiful significance of it and to put it into words to explain to other humans how this wonderful process continues to work and maintain you all in your physical bodies.

So now we leave you Malcolm. We thank you for getting a new tape recorder making it possible for us to transmit this information to you. We hope that you can transcribe it into words quite quickly and put these parts into your book as an explanation for all the things that are perceived as miraculous on this planet Earth. Thank you, Malcolm. Thank you for doing this work with us. We know you love this work, we hear you say so in your prayers and we are overjoyed that you are so happy to take part in this great enterprise. We thank you, we love you and we send you our blessings. Goodbye from us all now.

Since transcribing that communication my Guides gave me – June 15, 2009 – the following statements to add to the communication:

- *Element transmutation is common to all life forms.*
- *Not only humans but plants and animals use love energy to manifest required atoms.*
- *This information should be added to Angel communication about transmutation.*

Malcolm K. Smith / June 13, 2009

Appendix 7: Angel Communication, July 20, 2009

Hello Malcolm, yes we are here ready to talk to you again. Thank you for your request for more information about the fractals and the power of the images that come from them and the energy in the images. We are going to tell you today about a single process which you saw by coincidence (haha!) in that cartoon on television today. That cartoon was showing the story from China about a little boy – Shouping in the original story – who had the ability to draw pictures and then those pictures would come to life and create reality. That is the basic idea of what we are talking about today that people can create pictures by drawing, painting and taking photographs. There is energy put into those pictures that can, under certain circumstances, come into reality with a four-dimensional effect.

That is what happens when artists paint pictures. You are already familiar with the idea that when they do that spiral energy is put into the painting. Now we are telling you that this is just a special case of a very general effect that is possible in all known creation.

This gift comes to us from God. God created the universe by imagining it. If you like He drew a picture of the universe. By feeding the infinite energy that is God into the picture He was able to create the physical form of the universe which is much more than humans are able to comprehend. But you feel easier talking about physical things on the scale of your galaxy and solar system so that is where we will confine our talk today.

The energy that comes from God through Sirius which is stepped down in power so that it is useable by humans is absorbed by humans as we discussed. It is absorbed by their merkaba and their carbon atoms with their tetrahedral structure. In addition it is absorbed by the cosmic lattice which is throughout the universe – all twelve dimensions of it. As you know it is around your planet and humans can access the energy in the lattice either with the help of their higher selves to create new things for the Earth or humans can have access to the energy on an unconscious basis to create their future reality.

In this second process the lattice energy is absorbed by people unconsciously and without help from their higher selves. It is an automatic process that feeds through humans and the results depend on how they feel and the energy level that they send out to resonate with the lattice. You have covered all these things in your book so far.

You are starting to think about other ways in which people use that lattice energy. When they create something, a painting, a piece of music or an invention, then their higher self helps them put spiral love energy into the thing that they have created. Its energy is available to affect other humans, although those other humans are not aware of the process by which their emotions are stirred. The most familiar example, as you have already stated, is music. When people listen to music it bypasses their intellectual apparatus and goes straight to their heart and gives an emotional response. That is the same sort of thing that happens with paintings, great acting performances, poetry, photography and other aspects of art. In each case the human that is creating something is working with their Golden Angel – the same being as their higher self – to create an energy picture which is like a template which we told you we Angels send down to Earth to create various things. We have talked about the templates that give rise to the crop circles and the templates that produce miraculous pictures on walls and cloaks and many other natural objects of your civilization. All those manifestations of that energy are there as witness to the love energy that All That Is sends to all the universe.

The artists that are taking information/energy from the lattice and with the help of their Golden Angel putting it in to the work of art, whatever that may be, those artists are merely following in the footsteps of All That Is. Humans and Angels are divine creatures and have the same access to energy from All That Is. Angels create templates to bear witness to this fact. Humans are becoming aware that when they create something they put into that creation the energy of All That Is so they too are bearing witness, they see it as witness to beauty and order and consciousness. When you write a book, such as yours Malcolm, you put energy into every page and that is a very good way to bear witness to the love that comes from All That Is.

That is the basic process that you touched upon and you wished to enquire about. Now we tell you more about the structure of that energy and how it manifests itself in different dimensions, what you call fractional dimensions or fractals. When someone creates a fractal picture – like Cheryl Harnish, an artist working in Vancouver – the energy of the fractal painting manifests as a spiral and that spiral can be detected by pendulum or other dowsing means. (I have seen this demonstrated -MKS)

You have seen in that book by Laszlo that some dowsers don't necessarily have to create a picture but they can construct in their minds through imagination a template – maybe it's just a triangle or a three-dimensional shape. We are telling you now that the construction is in the 5th dimension and that energy construct can be detected by other dowsers with their pendulums or their rods.

All these examples we are touching on this afternoon are offshoots of the same basic concept; that conscious beings can produce energy constructs – which you refer to as templates – and those templates are at the basis of works of art. The energy constructs of the works of art by humans mainly exist in the 5th dimension but they project their power into your four dimensions that you inhabit and that is the picture that you see. Earlier your Guides told you about energy tides in the 5th dimension creating beautiful patterns in your space-time that you call nebulae – that is the same process. The dowser or the artist or Angels construct in the 5th dimension an energy template and that is projected into your space-time continuum and manifests itself as some physical thing, maybe a painting, maybe a piece of music. Maybe even a human, because we have told you already that humans are projections of templates that Angels have created. The Golden Angel creates the template and projects the energy into the four dimensions of Earth and it manifests as a human being.

It's all a question of projection and the analogy that we use here is that you can project on a screen a three-dimensional image – the third dimension being the depth of the picture which is constructed by artistic means such as perspective but in actual fact it is only two dimensions that you see on the screen. As you go mentally into the picture on the screen the two dimensions become three dimensions as you become part of the picture yourself. At some point you are half immersed in the picture and half still looking at it as two dimensions and that is where the concept of fractional dimensions comes from. In that case your scientists would say you are at a fractal dimension of 2.5.

The mathematics of fractal dimensions are quite obscure to most humans, although they see them as beautiful patterns. In fact they are usually generated by computers from a simple equation that gradually winds you along a spiral that goes from the four dimensions in which you live to the 5th dimension. That is what is happening in the pictures and the music, you are presented with spiral energy that you put into the painting. As you travel along that spiral you move along an axis that brings you from two dimensions to three dimensions to four dimensions and eventually to the 5th dimension.

The energy spiral exists in the 5th dimension down to your four dimensions that you call space-time. The energy spiral is a way that you can access the 5th dimension – it passes through the veil. The veil is getting thinner all the time due to the planet's energy changes, soon it won't be there at all and we will have a much closer connection with you. Until that happens in a few years the energy spirals that you create in your pictures, your paintings and your music are like access tubes. By traveling down the spirals you can go into the 5th dimension and information can come from the 5th dimension into your four dimensions where it manifests itself as something such as a painting. But the concept of the painting, the basis of it, is in the energy that creates the spiral.

That is why your theory of abstraction looks at traveling into paintings along the spiral to see where the effects are. You have already glimpsed the mechanism, it's as if a two-dimensional painting you are looking at has sticking out of it a four-dimensional spiral that leads into the 5th dimension.

You can travel in and out of that 5th dimension by moving along the spiral. As you move along the spiral so it gives rise through the mathematics to forms that are recursive – that is from one layer of forms to the next we have the same shape of form but they are at a different size. (Recursive means a math expression each term of which is determined by applying a formula to preceding terms -MKS) It's like looking at an aerial view of a piece of coastline, we see bays and promontories and then as you come closer to the coastline you see that it is made up of smaller bays and promontories and we can go right down to a scale where individual rocks and pebbles form those apparent bays and promontories. As you know this is the basis of the fractal dimensions and at any point in the spiral, down those different sizes, as you approach the 5th dimension you can produce forms. For example in your four dimensions you can produce natural forms such as plant material and clouds. Those are two examples of manifestation of the fractal energy somewhere along that spiral.

In the video *Colors of Infinity* that you have this is explained well and we recommend you to watch this again and you will get a feel for how those recursive shapes occur again and again at different levels as you go down the spiral. At some point in the spiral is the manifestation that you call plant – and you know trees have similar branching shapes – and all of that can be represented by mathematics as your scientists have discovered. Really it's not just at the level of your Earth plane that those are there, that same recursive shape is there at all different levels, all different fractal dimensions which are represented as you go along the spiral of energy from the 5th dimension that leads out into your four dimensions of space-time.

Where you see your tree forms you see some aspect of the template that All That Is has created for your Earth plane. All That Is conceived the idea of a planet called Earth and imagined those plants and animals that you have on your planet. He imagined them to exist at a certain level of dimensionality, at some point along the spiral energy that we are calling a template. These levels of appearance of plants and animals appear as fields of the energy that is traveling outward in a spiral form of a template. If at some point you stop the movement out along the spiral and you consider the energy that you have there it is in the form of fields. Those fields are the morphic fields that Rupert Sheldrake talks about. That is the natural existence of all the things that are manifested on the surface of the Earth which come from All That Is imagining those plants and creatures on the Earth.

You humans imitate that process because you are divine. You are part of God and have the divine spark within you. You are able to imagine similar templates. From your place in the four dimensions you project the energy spirals that create the templates up into the 5th dimension. So that the template energy is there at various levels and can manifest itself in any particular level in a pattern.

Your idea Malcolm about the level of abstraction is that you can take a picture and travel along its energy spiral and at various points along the spiral if you look at the fractal forms that are expressed there you will see something which is abstracted from the original representation of physical form in the painting. The further you travel along the spiral the manifestations of the energy become more and more abstract. That is what your theory says and you are quite right in expressing it. We want you to work on it but at a later date. For now we would like you to express your idea in your book because it will explain about those energy spirals that people detect in paintings and pictures. Later you can work with Michelle measuring those energies and showing how they change

228

as you move along the energy spiral to give greater and greater levels of abstraction. You move until you reach eventually in the 5th dimension a concept that is like the focus of the spiral and is where the artist's Golden Angel started the spiral when he helped a human bring the energy from the lattice.

That energy starts out as a concept and it is sent into the Earth plane along an energy spiral as it travels along the energy spiral it can at any point manifest different aspects of that idea. Those aspects can manifest as various things copying or simulating the creations of the past that All That Is has projected into the physical world.

We hope that has given you some idea of how this process works. It is a difficult thing for humans to imagine this but if you imagine the spiral as a stretched out Slinky spring you could put pictures along the spring maybe of a cloud. As you move down that spiral towards the 5th dimension you may see more basic forms of that cloud. As you approached the source of that energy you see the point at which All That Is has put the energy into the spiral flow, the concept or the original idea that was started by All That Is. As you get nearer that those cloud shapes become more basic, become less elaborate, more abstracted until they become one point when it reaches the 5th dimension. We hope that is a concept that you could model by having a Slinky spring extended with different pictures at points along the spring, each of those pictures would become simpler as you got near the end of the spring which is the origin, the idea of All That Is.

Now Malcolm we think that we should stop at this point. We have given you a concept which we believe you can work with. We know you are anxious to continue on with the chapter so if you can summarize what we have just told you in this section of your book it will be useful. Then this will serve as the basis for a program of research that you, Michelle and others can undertake in which you measure the energy. You will understand what it is that you are measuring in those pictures that Michelle can create because you understand how you initiated those pictures with respect to your

Golden Angels. Then we want you to put all that work together with your experimental results into another book that you already know about.

Now you want to imagine that spring with pictures placed along its length and all that it represents. We leave you with that image in your mind.

Thank you for taking these words and recording them. Thank you for searching for these words in the first place. We are very pleased that you want to know all about the structure of the universe that you find yourself in. You want to bring this to your fellow humans so that they understand how this part of the universe is so miraculous and such a blessing from All That Is.

Thank you Malcolm for taking our words and using them, for bringing them to your fellow humans. We wish you all the blessings that are ours to give. We leave you now with all our love.

Malcolm K. Smith / 22 July, 2009

Appendix 8: Angel Communication, September 12, 2009

Welcome Malcolm! We are so pleased to have you back in connection again with us in this way. Although you were in connection with us when you were in England and we had great opportunities to inform you of things you needed to know. We were pleased to see that you took notes on scraps of paper and you have collected those together.

Yes, you were right in thinking that this is the information we gave you as you sat in that crop formation in the middle of the English countryside in Wiltshire near Silbury Hill which is a very important landmark for that area. It is a symbol of an earlier civilization that was partly responsible for the structures you know as Avebury and Stonehenge. In those days men still remembered the knowledge they had gathered at the time of Atlantis. Although in a scientific sense they were not as developed as you are now and certainly were not as developed as the original Atlanteans were, nevertheless they had very strong spiritual/scientific knowledge which they applied. As you know pyramids were very important in those days and we have talked to you about the tetrahedral structures in a pyramid that make it into a machine which can focus hyper-dimensional energy as you have so well written about in your previous chapters. Silbury Hill was a more recent version of a pyramid, more recent in the sense that it was since the time of Atlantis. But it was probably about the same time that pyramids were being built in Egypt that Silbury Hill was constructed.

The people that lived in what you now call England were in communication with the people that lived in what is now called Egypt. In fact there was a worldwide connection between all these people. This was at a time of the recovery after the cataclysm that destroyed Atlantis when people started to recover from the great hardships they had endured. This was the time that led to the building of the second Atlantis on an island in the Atlantic near what you now call Gibraltar. This was a time of recovery, of remembering past knowledge and a time of rebuilding the Atlantean Empire but on a much more fundamental level. There was not the great ruling class and the magnetic temple of rejuvenation and all those very high flying scientific inventions that the Atlanteans had and used to their detriment.

This new Atlantis was a much purer society that dealt with metals, in particular bronze. Bronze was made with copper brought from the area where the glaciers had retreated after the last ice age. You know about that source of copper and how it was brought through Bimini to the new Atlantis. That led to what is now regarded as the bronze age.

In that time there was a world-wide network formed by people who went out from the new Atlantis. Those people went to areas where their past life brothers had lived and were now living in new bodies but had not had the benefit of guidance in developing simple technologies connected with farming and subsistence living. Those people who came to help were regarded almost as gods by the people that received the information. That's where the names came from such as Kukulcan and Quetzacoatl that were applied the bearded white men that came from the second Atlantis and helped people who were struggling to return to some form of civilization. All those people were connected with a worldwide network which understood the need for communication with other dimensions. They also understood that the hyper-dimensional energy that came to them was – as you say in your notes 'like food parcels from home.' They understood that their spiritual origins were in another dimension and they could receive energy from that dimension – from home – by constructing devices such as pyramids. That is why the pyramids were built in Egypt and why Silbury Hill was built in what is now Wiltshire.

You Malcolm were connected with that age as you understood previously. You were one of the Kukulcans that traveled in the self propelled boats – boats without oars as the native people recorded

232

– and you helped people understand about farming, growing crops and creating craft objects like pottery and textiles. That is why you are so interested in that type of work in this lifetime. When you were young you used to help people in the technology network (MKS: for example people in third world countries) and you gave advice in making simple craft objects such as textiles and paper. – In that past lifetime you were part of that network that spread out first around the Atlantic and eventually the whole world. You traveled to places like Silbury Hill and Avebury so this lifetime's visits are certainly not the first, you have been there many, many times in other lifetimes.

That was one of the reasons why we chose to guide you to the crop formation in that location, near Avebury for one thing, and the other thing that was significant was the crop formation have been given the name 'The Weave' which related to your connection with textiles and those skills which you imparted to more primitive people. You helped them come into a more craft oriented world where they had objects and knowledge about farming, agriculture and cultivation and use of the materials made with those skills. That is the background to why that particular crop formation was selected for you. You were right in thinking you could see other crop formations as you approached Avebury from those hills but we wanted you to go to that particular one we had chosen. It was particularly significant too that it was under the white horse carved out of the hillside above the crop formation. (MKS: I was directed by the people in the Avebury 'Henge Shop' to another formation which was more in the form of a spiral but I got 'lost' on the road and was directed to the Weave by two people I met in a roadside parking place.)

Now we come to the information that we told you while you were kneeling in that crop formation and you felt the energy all around you and you heard some sounds which were indications of our presence. The information we wanted to tell you was about how the human body is just a vehicle – a very sophisticated, skilled vehicle but nonetheless just a vehicle. You were quite right in your discussion of the two I's (letter I's) in thinking of the true power behind the body as being the human spirit. You are right in thinking that the human spirit comes directly from its home in what you regard as the 5th dimension. It is free to roam over many dimensions when it is in what we shall call its ground state, that is your normal state when you are between lifetimes on any planet.

You are right in thinking that spirit has all the powers of a sentient being, it reasons, it remembers, it makes plans, it looks through other lifetimes and it learns through its experiences in those lifetimes. We will not go into the time element here because it is quite complicated. Basically all the lifetimes are happening simultaneously but for your Earth brains that is a difficult concept to imagine and so we will talk about past and future lives because that is the way you humans think about these things. We will work within that framework so you do not become confused. When you are in spirit, without a body, then all you have to do to think about something is to touch upon the relevant part of the cosmic lattice. All the memories are stored in the cosmic lattice and you resonate with the lattice – we all do that. If you need to think about some particular item, what you on Earth call strawberry jam, for example, just the mere idea of something like that leads you to the part of the cosmic lattice where the information on strawberry jam is residing and resonating. You are able to resonate with it and that becomes a thought. You have the ability to recall those thoughts – what you call on Earth memory. All those powers are available to the human spirit.

When a spirit decides to come into a physical body for a lifetime on a planet, and there are many different forms of physical bodies that can be taken, some very solid and others only partially solidified – as you know all bodies consist of energy. When a spirit decides to take on a body it selects parents who will conceive the body and the spirit is helped into the body as a human. (Guides' note added while transcribing: Refer to the description of conception given earlier and the role of DNA.) One thing about the body – the spirit is not trapped in it, it is not a prisoner in the body, it is quite free to

234

leave and go and explore other parts of the four dimensions where you live or other dimensions. In doing so you call it an Out Of Body Experience. Some people are quite skilled in going out of body such as the remote viewers that you read about. Sometimes people come out of their bodies spontaneously as a result of medical emergencies.

You yourself Malcolm have experienced spontaneous leaving of the body, not as a result of a medical emergency but because it was time for you to experience that. You knew how to do those things before you came into the body. In fact you have often wondered about the point at which you came into your body. Your spirit, Malcolm, did not come into your body at the time of your birth on 12 November, 1936, but it came in a few months later because your spirit was already engaged in activities in Spain on your planet Earth. Your spirit had to finish those activities before it was free to come into the body which is known as Malcolm Kenneth Smith. You have a memory of that moment when you entered the body and we think you can recall that scene that you saw as a spirit as you entered the body. We remember that you were a little uncomfortable at first in that body because it seemed, after your freedom of being in spirit for a while, it was almost like being put in a prison. But you knew that was only a temporary thing while you were a child. You soon learned to come out of that body in what you thought were dreams. In dreams people come out of body quite frequently, but sometimes they experience the dream while still in the body. So there a number of different ways that you can have those experiences that you remember the next morning as a dream.

One of the ways that you came out of the body was when you were trained by what you would call aliens or interplanetary beings – who are also inter-dimensional beings – and who travel between dimensions and help young humans learn about the existence which we all share. You remember being on the craft and the dreams you had about the experiences on the craft and in fact those were not dreams as such – although you remember them as that – but in fact they were out of body experiences. Your childhood colleague,

Marjory, traveled in those same craft with you. You remember each other from being in the craft together with several other children being shown wonders of the universe. You understood so much of what was happening around you in the world from a spiritual point of view. You, Marjory and the other children learned your spiritual lessons while you were in physical body on Earth.

So you are quite familiar with traveling in spirit form and that is why you are quite correct when you say the human has two I's, two personalities perhaps, although that is a word with meaning that we don't want to involve here. Let us say there are two beings that exist: one is a physical being – the body that you recognize and which so many humans regard as 'me.' When they say "This is me," they mean they are the body. But you are quite right in pointing out that the true 'me' is the spiritual one that inhabits the body as a vehicle. It is quite analogous to getting into a car – the driver is the spirit.

When the spirit steps into a body it is just like the diver stepping into a car. But it is a very sophisticated car that tends to think it is the boss, but in actual fact it is a very elaborate computer that the spirit manipulates in order to experience physical life. Sometimes that spiritual being becomes a little lost in the drama in which it is taking part as a human body and we want you Malcolm to point out that the spirit is the true 'me' in the human body. That true 'me' is the spirit that came from the 5th dimension and all the roles the body can play are valuable lessons but they should not be confused with being the true existence.

Another analogy that comes to us is actors in a play. The actor is the spirit that comes to the theatre and puts on a costume and takes a part in a play. That is what you do when you come from the 5th dimension as spirit and enter a body, you put on a costume. You are taking part in a play on the surface of the planet Earth. You learn from that experience of being in the play and interacting with the other people, the other beings on the planet. Some of the beings are Angels although you do not always recognize them as

236

that but sometimes it's necessary for a critical part in the play to come forward then an Angel will appear as a human. You have experienced this quite recently with the man that came to your talk a few months ago (MKS: Talk at ISA) who reminded you about zero point energy – you realized that he was an Angel. Sometimes it's necessary for an Angel to come along and give a hint to one of the actors in the play as to how the play should develop, that's what was happening in that case.

The important thing to remember is while you are on the surface of this planet, while you are in the play, <u>it is only a play</u>. It is not the whole game, it is not all that there is, because after the play is over you take off those costumes – what you call die – then you go back to your spirit existence with all the memories of the time in the play. The experiences you gained in the play are still with you. So your true 'brain,' your true understanding resides in your spirit. The physical brain of the body you occupy is just a very elaborate, very wonderful, very miraculous computer that you learn to operate as a spirit driver or as a spirit actor.

Sometimes in that play some people take on the part of a villain and they may do something very bad such as kill someone else but that is necessary for the play to progress and for other people to learn from that. When the actors gather after the performance and have a party and laugh about interactions, then the murderer often chats with the murdered person and they both understand what it is that they had to do with each other while they were in the play. Other than the experience that was gained the play is over now and the actors have gone back to their dressing rooms. They celebrate, they think what a wonderful experience it was but they are glad they are not in the play all the time. Because that is what many people on the planet Earth at the present time are suffering from, they are trapped in the play. As Kryon says, "They think the camouflage is real!" We know that the camouflage is just part of the scenery on the stage. The actors are wearing costumes to make them look like regular humans. But if they give some thought to it they realize that they all have experience beyond the play when they go back to become spirit beings once more.

There are a lot of people on the Earth at this time that do not want to think about these things. They think they are happy just experiencing the play and that's all they want, they don't want to think beyond that. That's why Malcolm we want you to write about these things, to acquaint people with their true reality. Where home is, where they will go after their part in the play is over. So we would like you to write a chapter in your book about this, using the information we have given you. You already understand a lot of this and you started to write about it such as the demonstration of Adam's out of body experience. His memory of what he experienced is an excellent example for you to use. We strongly suggest that you keep that in your chapter as convincing proof of the memory and the thinking ability of a human spirit when it is out its body, or out of its vehicle, or out of its theatrical costume.

So all these things we have told you came to you while you were kneeling in that crop circle. We have explained the historical connections with that area and with that concept of the crop formation. While you were kneeling there all these ideas were implanted in your spirit. It came to you, if you are interested, in a ball of light that traveled across the fields but you were not able to see that ball of light. It wasn't until the evening when you read that book that talked about ball lightening and balls of light that you recalled that experience that you had in the Royal Marine cadets. You were on parade and it rained and there was a thunderstorm and a ball of light came and touched you. Everyone was in awe of you and thought you had been electrocuted but you were quite peaceful about it. There was no problem. That was an early example of information being given to you about your life path. When you were kneeling in the crop formation a similar event occurred but you did not notice the ball of light that came to you. So your Guides arranged for this reminder about the Royal Marine cadet experience to be given to you. You very quickly asked your Guides about it and they made the connection with the crop formation ball of light.

We are happy that you knew what it was that you had to do when you set out that day to find a crop formation. We are very glad

238

that you were persistent and were able to follow your intuition that guided you past those other crop formations that were on the horizon but you knew they were not for you. We are pleased to see that you persisted in asking people where you had to go. Those people were put in your path to lead you to that crop formation called The Weave. Thank you for doing that and receiving this information from us. Now we feel we have given you all you need to finish the chapter you have already started about the two beings that constitute a human being. We suggest that instead of talking about the two I's, maybe you could use the words 'physical being' and 'spiritual being' as it may be more meaningful for your readers. We want you to get away from terms that could be mistaken for psychology terms because we don't want people to be confused. So we suggest you talk in terms of the two beings that fuse together to form what you call a human being.

Now Malcolm we think that we have given you enough for today. We will help you with other parts of the book. We are working to assure that the book is finished in good time. We hear your prayers for help about that and we will do all we can to bring about a hasty completion of the book – but not too hasty, we want it to be of the highest possible quality so we don't want you to rush anything. Just take your time and explain all these items as we have given them to you today. Now we leave you Malcolm with love and blessings that are ours to give from all of your Angels that are around you all the time. We love you, we thank you for all your help. Goodbye.

Malcolm K. Smith / 14 September, 2009

Appendix 9: Angel Communication, October 4, 2009

Hello again Malcolm! How happy we are to see you so ready and prepared to do this again. We are happy to see that you feel happy about this work as well. We know you love this work you do on the book and you will enjoy learning about the new aspects of the human existence so it brings us great happiness to see you working like this and receiving this information with open arms.

Today we are going to tell you about the structure of the human quantum field and how all the things you have been writing about in the last few days work together to produce this thing that you call human consciousness. We have to start with the light that is issued from all the cells of your body. Yes, even the blood cells as they move around your body are giving off light as well. As your scientist Popp found all human cells – and all living cells too for that matter, in plants as well as animals – give off light. In the human body – which is what we will be talking about for the rest of the time today – that light travels between the cells as a form of communication. It is a very precise, exquisite form of communication because it depends on the tiny openings in the cell walls called tubules – at least that's what humans call them. That light travels from the cell interior where it is generated by cellular reactions through the tubules so that all the cells join in one great body-wide communication. This communication consists of one great standing wave of light. The light from the cells resonates throughout the structure of the human body creating a standing wave of light.

The frequency of that vibration depends on the state of mind of the human – as we will see you can change that frequency by the way you think about your world and your existence. If you are in a happy state of mind – as you are now Malcolm – then that frequency is high. You speak of your vibrations being raised. That's what has happened to you in the last fifteen minutes since your Guides told you we would give you this information. If you are in a poor state of mind as a result of sadness or bad news, or even worse depression, then your vibration frequency is low. That is what is meant by 'feeling low' it means that the vibration rate of the light standing wave in your body is at a low frequency.

You can change that as you know from the things you have been told by Beth and many others who have written books about this sort of thing. You can change your rate of vibration by one of several strategies. The one that we always recommend to people when they are starting out in this area is by being thankful; by showing gratitude for your present situation. Nothing works so well to raise the vibration rate of the light in your body like being grateful for your existence. You are very good at this Malcolm, you give thanks every day for your existence and the wonderful things that are happening to you as you follow your life path. So your vibrations are very high nearly all the time. Not all the time you still have a few things – that are part of the human condition – that bother you and drag you down at times. Sometimes some outer negative influences work to bring you down but you have developed ways to overcome those, mainly through meditation. You are able to bring your vibrations back to their normal high level.

Now we have this standing wave of light vibrating right throughout the length of your body. The light travels to all the living cells in your body except your hair and finger and toe nails because after they leave the cells that generate them they no longer have the light in them. That light is in every part of your body that is alive, right to your finger and toe tips. You know that you can give it a further boost by absorbing energy as you do in your walking meditation. But that is another story and we will not digress into that now.

This light that vibrates throughout your body is what we call – and humans have started to call – the human quantum field. It is the home of your spirit while you are on Earth. Your spirit is energy, as you know. That energy of the human spirit combines with the energy that is vibrating in the form of light and the two together become the complete human quantum field. As you know the spirit has consciousness. It is energy that is aware of itself and that is what we call consciousness. The spirit is aware and revels in the joy it finds at being able to exist in the form of a human and experience life in a physical situation on a planet called Earth. But there are many other planets where spirits live in similar vehicles for the enjoyment and the learning that they can achieve in those physical worlds. Spirit moves through this quantum light field and attends to the heavenly needs of the body.

The physical needs of the body are taken care of by the physical being that comes into existence at birth. The human spirit does not need to attend to the body because, as you have described before, it is like an automatic computer controlled machine. It is very subtle and sophisticated and is able to care for itself and do many of the things that spirit needs it to do with great precision. We have talked about this before in that if you wish your body to throw a ball or shoot an arrow the detailed calculations of how to hold the body in order to maximize the effect of those actions is best left to the body. It has – as you would call it in your technology terms – an automatic guidance system. It is quite capable of directing a projectile to a particular target with great accuracy. You have experienced that yourself Malcolm and you recognize that is the mechanism that is generally referred to as Zen.

Those are requirements of the body which are subsidiary to our present discussion. This information we are giving you is about how the spirit interacts with the human quantum field. We must say before we go much further that the spirit does not have to stay within the quantum field. As you have experienced the spirit is quite able to leave the quantum field of the body and travel to other parts of the planet, to other planets or even to other times within your four dimensional space-time. The spirit has the flexibility and the freedom to travel and then it can return to the body that it occupies if that is what is required. But sometimes when a spirit leave its body it does not return and that is the event you call death. But most of the time when you go on an out of body experience – an OBE as you call it – you expect to return and you do so.

Some people have seen a silver cord that connects the living body to the spirit. When the spirit is away from the body that silver cord stretches out through the cosmic lattice and keeps the body and spirit connected. That is the same effect that your physicists call quantum entanglement (Einstein's 'spooky action at a distance' -MKS) because they see a similar kind of connection between sub-atomic particles that have interacted in some way. But we will not digress into atomic physics at present. We just note these things in passing.

Now we want to talk about, when the body is functioning well, how the spirit operates the body through the quantum field. In that book *The Field* – which is quite correct in most of its details – you were given the analogy of the Internet which you understand is an overall result of many computers joining together. You could say that the effect of all the cells in your body joining together through this light field has the same effect as an internet which is created in your body. The light interacting between the trillions of cells in your body is just like the electronic communication between all the computers on the Internet.

The spirit knows where all the web sites of interest are. That's because the spirit creates many of those web sites of interest by forming parcels of energy in the quantum field which vibrate with a certain frequency. These are connected with the cosmic lattice of course. There is complete connectivity between each human quantum field and the cosmic lattice. The spirit in any particular body forms nodes of energy and in that energy is stored the information about an event or object and that is what you call a memory. Just as you have memory sites in your computer so the human spirit forms – what we will call – web sites for each individual memory that is stored in the overall human memory.

The human brain has a physical representation of that internet stored in it. This is the physical part of the memory system. Let us say that each memory that is stored in the quantum field has a physical counterpart in the human brain. That is the part of the

244

memory, which includes instructions and past training, which the body uses when it performs routine tasks. A good example that you touched on once was learning a musical instrument. The human spirit decides that it would like to express emotions in the form of sound waves which you call music. It puts the thought into a quantum internet web site that the body should acquire an instrument and practice it. The body, especially one that is happy and joyful, readily agrees to do this. Physically it acquires an instrument and starts to practice. The spirit helps the body with the practice and receives energy from the music that is created and that energy is passed through the body. That is why you always feel warm when you play your instruments. That is the physical effect of the energy that comes through the music. As the body becomes more proficient at playing the instrument more and more memories are created; the memories of each of the tunes that the body learned. First of all the spirit records those memories in the quantum internet and a reflection of those memories are stored in the physical human brain. This means that the body has the capacity to play the instrument automatically. The body has at its disposal in the brain's memory cells a knowledge of all the tunes that have been practiced and the body can, quite automatically like a machine, reproduce those tunes on the instrument. But that is rather a bland, soul-less piece of music to other humans and it is not until the spirit's quantum memory unites with the brain's physical memory that the true spiritual emotion of the music is expressed in physical sound. The very best of the spirit and the body combines in situations like this to produce those memories both spiritual and mental and when those are aligned it is a very powerful source of beauty that stirs emotions in other humans as they receive that message of love. That's what music is, a message of love.

We have explained how the brain is set up with memories by the spirit. When the body is first given birth it has no memories. It is not until the spirit comes into the body – which usually is at the time of birth but may be delayed as you know – that it starts to create those memory nodes in the quantum field. It starts to build its quantum internet which constitutes spiritual memory which is reflected by physical memory. The child starts to learn how to walk and speak and builds its physical memory on which it can rely for automatic processing. When the human is undertaking creative work, such as writing a book, then it relies to a certain extent on physical memory, for example how to spell words. But for its concepts – its higher thoughts – it depends on spiritual memory. To access the spiritual memory the spirit moves about in the quantum field touching on those memory nodes that it has created – in a way it is like a human clicking on web sites on the Internet. The spirit can move very quickly – much faster than the speed of light, faster than humans can comprehend – over the quantum field internet and touches on those nodes of memory that it has created. The human brain understands those memories as it receives them and translates them into words that are eventually put down on paper so that other people can read them.

That is the process that we are doing with your spirit right now Malcolm. We Angels are combining together with your spirit and putting new memory nodules into your quantum internet. These are like new web sites – one for each small concept. Those will remain in your memory but you will need some prompting and so the body transfers those spiritual memories into physical memories in the form of words which you speak and are recorded by your machine. You can then process that at your leisure and put it on paper so that you can refer to it and use the concepts to write your book. We want you to realize that the concepts we bring you are first stored in your quantum internet as those memory nodules and the spiritual quantum internet pattern is copied into physical form in transient memory long enough for it to be put into words. All the parts of the message that are given to the quantum internet are faithfully stored – nothing is lost. The essence of that is transferred into your physical memory so that after this experience of channeling you can recall some of the essential parts. Probably not all the details are remembered because it is not necessary since you transcribed the memories into words which were recorded by your machine. This is how the memory works.

You were quite right in your recent writing that when the body needs to recall something – like the name of the street where you had to turn to the lake – then the spirit activates the quantum internet memory to provide some clues to assist the physical memory. But those clues the spirit provides are different to those that the physical brain uses to recall things. Whereas the physical brain recalls in terms of names, words and numbers the spirit recalls in terms of concepts. That is why the concept that was given in the example was of a misty island with knights riding down paths to the beach. That was the memory cue that was given from the quantum internet memory and that provided a clue to the physical body but it wasn't until the body saw the name of the street – Avalon – that it made the connection. Of course this was a demonstration of that process in action and your body received that information with great joy and recognized the value of the demonstration for understanding the mechanisms. We are in an unusual situation – as Beth said – it seems that the body is writing the book but really spirit is writing about itself and how it interacts with the body. For the book we are describing the processes that we are actually using to describe the processes. This is a strange loop structure again and as a result of the self reference this explanation gains great power.

It seems that we have covered all the aspects that we wanted to describe today. Besides being a strange concept for humans to consider, this is a relatively simple process. Like all things in the universe nothing is very complex. Your physicists would make it complex because they replace spiritual understanding by mathematics. They do that because they know how to manipulate the mathematics but they do not know how to manipulate the spirit. Besides which many of them do not acknowledge existence of the spirit. The result is the concepts – that come from their spirits – are expressed in mathematical form and in this form the body can manipulate those concepts. The difficulty with that is the body does not understand the results of the mathematical manipulation. Although the body – of the physicist – obtains equations which describe certain aspects of the universe, a true spiritual understanding of those concepts is not arrived at by that process.

It is necessary for people to learn by analogy and by example rather than acquiring knowledge through numerical manipulation. For example in the case of the Avalon memory 'nudge' that we provided, maybe it would be possible for the physicists to describe the concept of a misty island with knights riding down the paths to a beach as some numerical display. They could probably manipulate this display mathematically but they would never arrive at the single word 'Avalon.' That's a parallel to the attempts they are making to understand the concepts of the universe that they think are being fed to them by the numbers they arrive at and the imagination they use in trying to interpret the numbers.

One more thing that we should touch on – your Guides have already explained this – the shape of the quantum field is more or less fitted to the body. However, it extends outside the body to a certain extent particularly on the right side of the brain with most humans. This is because the spirit interacts most closely with the right side of the brain and traditionally that is where you get your mystical experiences, your artistic, creative thoughts. The spirit spends more time on the right side and less time on the left side of the brain because the latter is where physical thoughts, control mechanisms and physical processing of the requirements of the human body take place. All the physical activities are dealt with in the left side of the brain.

So as your Guides explained you can imagine the energy of the vibrating light quantum field – when it is occupied by the spirit – right throughout the body but there is a preponderance of energy over the right side of the brain. In most cases psychics do not see this as part of auras because much of the extra energy is expressed in other dimensions. Spirit connects with other dimensions through this part of the quantum field. The best way to regard this is as an electron cloud in a molecule. As you know, being a chemist, the electron cloud forms into orbitals (Which have the function of bonding atoms -MKS). There is a greater probability that an electron will be found in one of the orbitals than in the rest of the molecule. The orbitals can be visualized as protuberances sticking

248

out from parts of the molecule. The human quantum field is very similar in this respect in that it has a protuberance, or an orbital, over the right side of the brain. This means that there is a greater probability that the spirit will be found in the region of the right side of the brain than in any other part of the body. But of course the spirit occupies all cells of the body, and is present everywhere in the body. It is all a question of probability of where you would be most likely to find the spirit if you were able to look.

You can regard the complete human body as a two layer structure. The first layer consists of the molecules that constitute the cells that make up the physical tissue – that is the matter part of the body. Diffused completely through that is the second layer – an energy field that consists primarily of light, and that light is what we call the human quantum field. The human spirit comes into that quantum field and lives in it most of the time. It forms nodes of memory which are in effect an energy structure paralleled by the Internet structure that you have on Earth. The spirit can touch on any of the quantum nodes – corresponding to web sites – and activate memories which are translated into physical form in the human brain. So basically it is a two layer system; one physical and one spiritual and the two work beautifully together.

As the physical body gets older and the spirit becomes more experienced it travels more out of the body. Then you reach a point where it seems that there is no spirit present in the body much of the time. This is the stage that people get to with advanced age – as they approach 100 years of age, maybe some much earlier than that – in which their spirit is not present in the body most of the time. Then the body has difficulty recalling from its physical memories many things because the spirit is not there to prompt it. This is the stage that humans go through called dementia which is a precursor to death usually – not always but in many cases. Not all humans go through that stage, some retain the full connection between their spirit and their physical memories right up to the incidence of their death of old age. There are many different possibilities depending on the requirements of the particular human and the experience that it intends to gain while in schoolhouse Earth.

Now we think we have given you an account of this phenomenon with several different ways of looking at it. You should be able to use the material to complete your final book chapter about the interaction of spirit and humans. We know you have another chapter to write about the crop formation experience but that is just a matter of writing an essay and you already have all the material for it. It is just like an appendix but we suggest you write this as another chapter because the message we brought is very appropriate for humans on Earth at the present time.

Now we leave you Malcolm with thanks for doing this for us, for translating the spiritual memories into physical memories in the form of words and writing them on paper so that you can use them. We are very happy that you have developed this ability and we have this interaction process between us so that our concepts, our thoughts can be put down in a book for the benefit of other people who do not talk to Angels like you do. We love you Malcolm and enjoy being in communication with you like this and giving you information which we know you will value, be thankful for and will use to help your fellow humans.

Now we wish you goodbye with all our love, with all the blessings that are ours to give you. Until the next time we meet, we love you. Goodbye.

Malcolm K. Smith / October 9, 2009

Appendix 10: Angel Communication, October 17, 2009

Hello again Malcolm. Welcome to this probably final session that we need to bring to you before you complete your book. You have done very well in preparing it so quickly especially the last two chapters and we are very pleased with the progress you have made. We assure you that you will be very successful in getting your book published. We are very grateful that it is all working out so quickly so that your book can see the light of day by the start of 2010 which is where we wanted it to be when we set out on this mission.

As you heard before - but you didn't realize - we are the Crystal Light group that has been talking to you several times over the last few years. You first channeled for us in 2004 and at that time you thought we were a group of Guides, which was a reasonable assumption but in actual fact we are Angels. There is a very large group of us and we call our selves Crystal Light because that is meaningful to you. We remember that at the time we introduced that name you were using a crystal as a pendulum and you saw beautiful refractions of the light from it and that name seemed very appropriate. That suggested the name to us. We don't mind if you want to mention that name in your book. It gives a more personal feeling to messages that come from a group such as ours.

Now we need to talk to you today and give you some suggestions about the introduction to your book. This is our main purpose in coming to you today. First of all we want you to follow along the lines that you set down yesterday – you had a preview of our message really – that this book is not a 'How to Live' book. As you correctly state others such as Kryon and Wayne Dyer have presented that sort of message very successfully. Your specialization Malcolm is in explaining how the processes – such as energy and matter interactions – which humans regard as physics take place. We see your role in explaining those spiritual energy and matter interactions. In fact that can be the sub-title of your book. Go with 'Spiritual Chemistry' but then put after it 'Mechanisms of Interaction of Spiritual Energy and Matter'. That is what your book is about.

That is the type of book that we want you – as a scientist – to put forth because you can explain these things clearly without the unnecessary words that many spiritual people use because they are not familiar with the technical terms as you are. For example we talked at length about molecular orbitals as electron clouds. Unless you had studied chemistry and understood that type of concept you would not be able to explain that in purely spiritual terms. So it is necessary for you as a scientist to make clear those concepts which are applicable in different areas. We have used the molecular orbital as an analogy for the distribution of spirit around the human body. Only a scientist trained in chemistry could make those comparisons. We are happy that you are able and agreeable to do this for us. As a result you can say that your book is a 'The Way Things Work' type of book after the series of books with that or similar titles. That's what we are really talking about: how Spirit works in the physical world. So that's the first concept.

Another concept we want to explain in your introduction is that this is a new way to gain information. Until now scientists in your Earth plane have relied on experimentation and mathematics. They used mathematical methods to set up concepts and then they manipulated those mathematical concepts to arrive at conclusions. But as we described in our last communication with you, although those methods have produced some results which could not have been arrived at without them, those methods have their limitations. The main limitation of the mathematical approach is that it is very difficult for the scientists to interpret the answer. Schrodinger's wave equation represented an example of that limitation that the scientists wrestled with for some time before they accepted the dead or alive cat analogy as an explanation. Now we are coming to concepts such as the distribution of the spirit in the human quantum field which cannot be arrived at by mathematics. This is one of the reasons most of your scientists keep away from these areas because they cannot see how to apply mathematical methods to such concepts as presence of the spirit. So it is necessary for humans to use other methods to arrive at explanations of how the physical world works.

You Malcolm are one of the forerunners in realizing that direct communication with us - with beings in other dimensions - is a most suitable way of arriving at those concepts. By talking to Angels you are able to obtain information about spiritual energy and how it interacts with the physical world. This is a comfortable concept for you to work with; you do not shy away from it because of your creative spiritual background. But many people will have difficulty, particularly those who do not believe in the existence of spirit. We assure you that this is the way of the future. The Spanish man who contacted spiritual beings to understand the history of the Knights Templar in Spain – you know the book we are referring to – was another forerunner that used this method very successfully in obtaining detailed information that was not possible to be unearthed from diaries and writings of people back at the time of the Knights Templar. By past life research - in that case – he was able to bring out into the world a lot of the thoughts and concepts that were about at the time of the Knights Templar and use that information. It was only through contacting other dimensional beings that he was able to arrive at that information. That was one of the reasons why we put that book before you to encourage you and let you see that you are not the first to try this method.

Similar methods have been used by other people who have done this kind of work. Another one that comes to mind was a man who wrote about Earth changes (and archeology in *We are the Earthquake Generation* -MKS) and he based that on spiritual communication about what had happened in the past and what was possible in the future. Those two people – we can't give you their names because we can't find them in your memory banks - but you know the instances we are referring to and we will leave it to you to track down those particular books if you wish to include that in your introduction.

Those are two concepts that we want you to explain. You can say of course that you started out to write a book about psychic phenomena and as the book progressed you were given more information from spiritual sources that changed the direction of the book. You realized that Crystal Light and your own Guides were directing you to write a book about spiritual energy and its interaction with matter. That is another concept how you started to write one book and it changed into another, believe us, that is quite a common event that happens with other spiritual writers.

Of course coming back to our previous comments about spiritual writers you know for example that *Jonathan Livingstone Seagull* was written by channeling and that was completely based on spiritual sources. That is a spiritual book of course and the people who read it find that acceptable to understand that. But the history book of the Knights Templar was a spiritually derived book – in part at least – and that was getting away from the spiritual topics of *Jonathan Livingston Seagull*. Your book is even further removed from that with your ideas about the physical world that have been conveyed to you by spiritual communications and yours is the first scientific book to be conveyed partly by this method. Of course it's not all spiritually sourced – you are using material that came from textbooks for example. The molecular orbital topic is a good example of that where you had to look up definitions of orbitals in a text book. It is a combined source of information that you are using your physical world's best records combined with an angelic source from other dimensions.

We have already covered that this is not a book of direction on how to live your life. Maybe we should say something about the types of people this book is meant for. This book is aimed at a very wide audience. Of course the main group of people who will want to read it with great interest will be the searchers after spiritual truth such as yourself Malcolm, for example the people that attend Kryon and other seminars and people that refer to themselves as light workers.

But it will also appeal to what we will call 'fringe' scientists - scientists who work with physical methods and yet go to church on Sundays and hear messages about Spirit. Often they seem to have

254

difficulty combining those two ways of thinking. We want to reach those people and tell them that the truths they hear in church are just as relevant to their work as their next experiment. They can get guidance for their experimental procedures and concepts from Spirit. This is not something that only Malcolm Smith is going to do. What we would like is that many scientists would come to these spiritual ways of doing research and understanding the physical world. We would like you to suggest that this is a new way of doing research. It is research assisted by other dimensions.

In some instances this was the technique that was used by – what you would call – extra-terrestrial beings on other planets. For example Malcolm , you know about planet Kuzalini in the Sirius double sun system – this is an example of Kryon's statement that double stars are more likely to have inhabited planets around them – Kuzalini is inhabited by four dimensional beings like humans. The scientists on that planet use spiritual communications as a way of furthering their physical science. You Malcolm have seen in your out of body travels some of their experiments which you feel are familiar to you. For example, you have seen those microscopic structures that look like bush shaped crystals that the Kuzalinian scientists were experimenting with. Those artifacts are connected with the spiral hyper-dimensional energy that you talk about in this book. You know that there is a connection with the bush-like crystal whisker structures you saw when doing your research at Manchester University. You don't know what that connection is just yet but it will be explained. As we produce more books along the same lines as 'Spiritual Chemistry' the connection will become clear and you will see experiments to do. What we would like is that the scientists of Earth emulate the scientists of Kuzalini in referring to spiritual sources for guidance in their experimentation. They will make progress much faster if they enlist the help of beings in other dimensions.

Some of the words that you have used in your book will need elaboration. You have a chapter that talks about physics and that is a very good way to explain the concepts. The concepts needed are generally at the secondary level of education in most countries of the world. What we are saying is that there are other concepts which are not familiar to earth scientists which will need to be explained. So we see in the future a text-book of spiritual science which describes phenomena, for example the bush crystal growths connected with hyper-dimensional energy, that are unknown on the Earth at this time. We will set a number of these things in a future book so that is something for you Malcolm to consider. You can be sure you have a long future ahead of you writing many books along these lines. Spiritual Chemistry is your first book and it will be followed by many more. You will become known for this.

Eventually people will come to accept this new way of doing scientific research. This new way of thinking and understanding the world that involves Spirit will explain so many things that are happening in the physical world that are unexplainable by accepted Earth science. For example the crop formations; people have this evidence placed before them, but as you say in your Chapter 8, many people – at least in England where you enquired – do not want to accept the existence of this information. The signs that appear in the fields are ignored or explained away as artifacts made by humans. You, Malcolm know that this is not true and you have started a trend by talking about it in your book. Why is it that so many humans insist on covering their eyes and not looking at the things that are presented to them. There are the crop formations, the orbs in digital photographs and the spiritual printing as you have called it.

{By the way we think that you should leave the section on your grandfather's picture in your book. When you first saw the photograph you readily accepted it but it wasn't until you went back to Portsmouth and saw that it was made of paper – an old notice that had been pasted on the door – that you started to doubt. But it doesn't matter what the material is that conveys the message; whether it was a pigment that had been put there miraculously or whether it was paper that was applied and then torn away. The fact remains that the image was created and conveyed to you a

256

message. So we think you should leave that in your chapter on spiritual printing. You can put in a footnote that it was explainable as paper stuck to the door but it's no different to a message being conveyed by a crop. You know that the material that is being worked on is growing wheat, or some similar crop, which is being modified to convey a message. The paper that was on the door of your grandfather's barn was like the crop; it was just a material that was there and could be modified to create a pictorial representation of an Angel. That's what it is; the Golden Angel or the oversoul of your grandfather George. So we would like you to leave that section in your book just as it is. You can add a note to say what we have just told you that the paper material of the picture is analogous to the material of the crop circles which convey so much information by their beautiful messages.}

{We are glad your course of action on that was turned. Your scientific purity was beginning to assert itself and we understand that, but if you look at it in the right way you see that it is just as miraculous as spiritual printing or a crop circle being formed in a few seconds.}

We have covered all the things that we wanted to tell you today. We would like you to set these things out plus you have a lot of notes and if you think of more things as you read through the notes then you can include them in your introduction. We think that is all we need to tell you today. We suggest you make the introduction short and snappy – as you would say – because this will be the thing that induces people to buy your book. They will probably be looking at it in a book store and wondering if it's something they need and they will look at the introduction to see what it's all about. So we suggest you keep the introduction quite short.

With that dear Malcolm we thank you. We will end at this point. We tell you once more how happy we are that you are prepared to do this work. We leave you now to complete your beautiful book and put it into the world's hands so that information can be shared among all humans that will listen. Thank you for helping us convey this information to the world. Thank you for working so hard and persistently in preparing the book especially over the last month you have really concentrated your efforts on it and we really appreciate the speed with which you have brought this thing to a conclusion. We leave you now with our thanks and blessings that are ours to give and our love. We love you Malcolm, we thank you and wish you goodbye.

Malcolm K. Smith / October 18, 2009

Index

264

Picture Credits

Figure 1-1	Courtesy of the Peabody Museum of Archaeology and Ethnology, Harvard University.
Figure 2-1	Copyright Klaus Monies, Vancouver.
Figure 2-2	Copyright Klaus Monies, Vancouver.
Figure 2-3	Copyright Klaus Monies, Vancouver.
Figure 2-4	Copyright Klaus Monies, Vancouver.
Figure 3-1	Diagram by Malcolm K. Smith.
Figure 3-2	Photo by Michelle DeMello.
Figure 4-1	Photo by Michelle DeMello.
Figure 4-2	Photo by Barbara Barraclough.
Figure 4-3	Photo by Malcolm K. Smith.
Figure 4-4	Internet anonymous photo.
Figure 5-1	Copyright Klaus Monies, Vancouver.
Figure 5-2	Photomicrograph by Malcolm K. Smith.
Figure 5-3	Copyright Klaus Monies, Vancouver.
Figure 6-1	Copyright Klaus Monies, Vancouver.
Figure 7-1	Courtesy of ELan Dubro-Cohen, The Energy Extension, Inc.
Figure 7-2	Diagram by Malcolm K. Smith.
Figure 8-1	Photo by Malcolm K. Smith.
Figure 8-2	Courtesy of Mark Fussell, The Crop Circle Connector.
Figure 8-3	Courtesy of Mark Fussell, The Crop Circle Connector.

LaVergne, TN USA
26 August 2010
194662LV00003B/15/P